There is no time like
HEAVEN

The Restoration of the Faith Circle

Scott Gulsvig

River City Press, Inc.
Life Changing Books

There is No Time Like Heaven
The Restoration of the Faith Circle
Copyright 2013, Scott Gulsvig
All Rights Reserved

ISBN: 978-1-934327-81-4
        1-934327-81-6

GRAPHICS: Rick Pollock

PUBLISHER:
River City Press, Inc.
P.O. Box 125
Siren, WI 54872
www.rivercitypress.net
publisher@rivercitypress.net

IN MEMORY OF...

JAY SUBSTAD and his wonderful love of Honduras. My friend, who I talk about throughout this book, died of a heart attack before I published this book.

DEDICATION
Thanks

I dedicate this book to Jeff Barber, a true friend. May he rest in peace. He was the original knucklehead that just loved everyone, and prompted me to seek answers and more out of life. I miss you dude! I truly cannot believe I wrote a book. This is parting of the sea stuff. I want to thank my wife, Keri and my kids, Kippen and Brenon for making me a better person. My Mom and Dad and brothers for a great childhood and my mother and father-in-law that just get it. I also want to thank Rick Pollock for doing the illustrations and believing I could do it. I wanted his name on the cover, but he eats humble pie everyday for breakfast. Also Bob Wolf and River City Press, his monthly phone calls drove me nuts, but he was always encouraging and never pushy. If you ever write a book call Bob.

Also thank everyone at PTM, Prayer Force, Small Group Bible Study, and everyone associated with Agua Viva for listening to my knucklehead stories and the cool staff at Hosanna that weekly teach us a way to follow God that truly includes the Holy Spirit, never judging just loving. Also my buddy Jeff for walks with Jazzi.

Without these connections this would have never happened, true connections.

Scott
A true knucklehead

Table of Contents

FOREWORD

June 22, 2011

Typically, the best person to compose a foreword to a book is an industry expert or someone famous to bring glitz and glory to the process. I am neither. I am a brother in Christ to Scott. I have known Scott for six years and I have been involved in a Bible study group with him through those years. Scott has become a great friend to me and I feel compelled to help him tell his story.

The reason I have such a strong feeling to help him is due to a tug on my heart from God. Scott has seen tremendous change through growth in his faith in Christ. It is through experiencing the changes I've seen in Scott that I am acting on what I consider to be a direct command from God. In fact, I am beginning to write this before he is even finished with his book and without him knowing that I've started. If it is God's will and Scott's desire, this foreword may not even end up in the book and will be nothing more than a private letter to Scott detailing the inspiration he is to me and many others.

As I have previously mentioned, Scott and I have been in a Bible study and have developed a great friendship over the past six years. In February of 2011, we had a mutual friend talk to us about his pending divorce from his wife. We were invited to participate in a prayer group on a Saturday morning. Scott called me to see if I was going to attend and pathetically, I said no. I indicated to Scott I would feel uncomfortable and awkward in that kind of setting with people I didn't know. Scott understood my feelings and indicated he wouldn't likely attend either. A few days later, Scott called me and told me that he went.

Scott will go into more detail on the events that surround the call on his heart to attend that prayer group, but the important truth is that he acted on that tug on his heart. As a result, God's kingdom has expanded in a way that amazes me every time I get an update.

I can't keep up with Scott. He is doing exactly what I believe we should all do; and that is to serve God and expand His kingdom. I believe many of us have moments where God tugs at our hearts and tells us to go in a certain direction or to help with a certain event. The problem is we tend to ignore those calls. I have as much experience as most in ignoring these calls, because as a product of Christian education from kindergarten through college graduation, I have countless recollections of times I've ignored a tug from God.

Scott chose not to ignore a call and as a result the Holy Spirit worked through Scott to transform the lives of so many that the magnitude of them can't possibly be traced. I am not proclaiming that joining a prayer breakfast will be the catalyst we all need to get the ball rolling, but to say that acting on God's requests of us will expand His kingdom and make our lives more profitable for God's calling.

I have never had an "aha" conversion moment in my relationship with Jesus Christ, my personal savior. I have gotten to know him slowly and with every set back along the way, our relationship has strengthened. Scott has a similar story and we've shared that with each other over the years. The advances to God's kingdom that have happened as a result of Scott attending a February prayer breakfast have not changed his Christian standing. Scott has not and is not looking for any greater personal return from God or that more glory should be shown to him than others. In fact, the humbleness that he exudes as he talks about his experiences is inspiring. Scott truly can do all things, through Christ, who strengthens him, as we all can. God's kingdom is at the center of this experience and expands as a result of God's work, not ours.

As you read this book, keep in mind that we become experts in Christianity by carrying out God's commands which He clearly defines in the Bible. We are not better Christians because we memorize one more Bible verse than our neighbor. We are not better Christians because we devote more time or donate more money to charity than our neighbor. We are better Christians because we put our faith in Jesus Christ who died on the cross to forgive our sins. It is through that faith that we commission ourselves to be a better influence on the world than it is on us. It is my prayer that we all react to the things God is calling us to do with our daily decisions. The influence we can have on each other is powerful and if we carry our actions out in God's name, we will expand His kingdom and further God's glory. To God be all Praise and Glory!

Benjamin D. Johnshoy
Shakopee, MN 2011

PREFACE

Before I start this book, I have to make a confession that makes the fact that I am writing a book even more amazing. I don't read, I don't write at all. I have maybe read 80% of one book in my entire life. I have a tough time reading a one paragraph email. As my friend Ben said in the forward, I am one of the most unlikely people on the planet to write a book. But, I know I wanted to share my story, and the effects it has had on my life. I have started to consider myself a restorer. Gabe Lyons in his book, "The Next Christian" calls people like me restorers. I don't have an agenda, I am not trying to preach, I am just sharing my story and how I have seen there is truly no time like Heaven, and that God does exist and the Holy Spirit is real. If I see you I am not going to preach to you, I am just going to tell you stories. Everyone likes a good story.

I am not writing this book for any credit, this book is not about me. It is a story of how the Holy Spirit came down and showed me some things that I need to share with others. I am not some wacko that would make up stories to put me out there, all the proceeds from this book are being donated to charity. Since this has happened to me, I don't pretend to be someone I'm not. I am still the same guy, I am changing slowly. Like my temper, I'm trying, just ask my wife Keri. And yes, I am self-centered and think of myself before others. I truly think the true purpose of this book is to show people how this is true stuff. It's as real as the back of my hand. And if you don't believe that's fine, I'm not going to push you or bug you. You are not stupid and I know that. I think that is where we as Christians are really missing the boat. We don't need to study and know the Scriptures inside and out in order to have the Holy Spirit rain down on us. I am NOT saying that isn't important. I am a proven fact that you just have to be open to the Holy Spirit.

I truly believe, in order to go through sanctification you need to have the Holy Spirit in you, which happens when you read Romans 10:9 and you believe it with all you heart. So at any point if it sounds like this book is about me, forget about it. I want to give all the Glory to God. This is just a series of events of God using an unlikely person, a person that would have never expected it. I am not going to say I don't have speaking or social skills. I am an extremely outgoing person and was in Toastmasters for many years, and I have been in sales my entire life. I have the gift of gab, so maybe I need to use that gift in the future, not sure but I am sure I will find out. I do know God chooses the most unlikely people, because He choose me to write this story, and these crazy events that are in this book. I think God is building an army of people that can restore this world to a place that shows we can all get along. Not a bunch of radical people, but some everyday people that said "yes," and God decided to have some cool things happen to them. Bringing Heaven down to earth, that is what it's really all about. Living our lives so we can tell others about our walks with the Holy Spirit and how He changes lives, and changes others around us. I am just bringing over a pie and telling some stories. I don't want anything, just to have you listen to some stories about what happened to me and some people around me. I am changing, I am asking people for forgiveness and trying to be more loving. But as a youth sports and pro sports watcher, I still yell at high school refs and get mad after a Viking's loss.

Also, the stories in this book are 100% true; I will be struck down as I stand here if one story is not the way it happened. That is what Jim Cymbala says, I want to just tell the story. We are all called to do something while we are on this earth, there is a giant plan we will never figure out, but we all have a purpose for the plan. I was a Christian and a believer before February 12, 2011. I have believed in Jesus and the Gospel story since college. I had heard the gospel many times before college, but on that day February 12, 2011 that is where it really stuck in my heart.

I was brought up in a church, going with my loving family. Sure, living under a roof with three boys had its days, but we all got along in the end and both of my parents put me on the right path and gave me a foundation of loving God. I still, to this day, live my life getting closer to what God has for us, but I am no way close to perfect. I am trying to live a good life, and love others, but it sure doesn't work that way for me every day. I fall short all the time, but I am also learning how to avoid sin with each asking moment. Though not sure why I am writing this, but I know as I write it just gets clearer. He just decided to take me from the waterboy to being on the football team and put me on the field for a bit. I am stepping on that field because He asked and I know He said, "Please!"

Let me make something perfectly clear, please understand this, I am a complete knucklehead. I do NOT have all the answers, I am not a preacher, I am nowhere close to perfect, I still go out with my buddies once and a while, and I still yell at my wife and throw mini tantrums like a 5-year-old when things don't go my way. You will read about the buckets in this book. My home bucket is getting better, not even close to perfect, but better. I am getting better at realizing my faults and things are slowly getting better. I also pray about it a lot, pray that I can keep a calm heart and really honor my wife. I know some stories of the Bible, but not near where I should be at this point in my life. So I am making this clear that I am a complete knucklehead, and I am still not sure why God choose me to write this book. But I know in my heart He did. In fact, a few of us at church are having fun starting a group called KFC, Knuckleheads For Christ. Joking, but not joking, just a group of guys that are honest and love the Lord.

Oh yah, one more thing, I am not good at punctuation and grammatical writing. I was terrible in English class. So if a word is misspelled or a period is out of place, please get over it. Remember, I am a big giant 6'-4" knucklehead. I am sure of one thing, I am 100% sure God wanted me to write this. So here goes, I hope you enjoy it. I know this book is about letting God be in our lives and being open to the Spirit that Faith in Him provides. I can't even begin to tell you how funny this is that I am doing this, some day we will meet and you will get the joke. I know that my journey and the connection to the Holy Spirit needs to be told. Today, more than ever, too many people are going through the motions and not looking to God's Spirit to make this world that we live in a better place. These stories are about the Spirit that lives in each one of us, who place our faith here on earth through prayer and have a relationship with Jesus. I am praying this book won't change me, hopefully I have enough good friends around me to keep me the way I am, living out my life daily as a husband, father, and a friend. When we live that way it brings us closer to Heaven, and brings the Spirit that brings peace and a tiny bit of understanding of Heaven with it. Just watch out, sometimes the Spirit brings a lot of Heaven. "There is no time like Heaven". Here goes.

I think I am one of the hundreds of thousands of people that have experienced life through stories that have truly moved me, and prompted me to write this book. I 100% believe that this is the power of the Holy Spirit, and that the Holy Spirit works in each and every one of us. I think there are a lot of people that are inspired every day, and for some reason God wants me to share mine. Maybe it is just an account to what has transpired in my life, or maybe a few people will read it and learn more of the Holy Spirit and His power. But I do know one thing, I am sure I have to write it!

CHAPTER 1

Losing the Faith
The Road to the Holy Spirit

1 Timothy 2:1 - *I urge, then, first of all, that petitions, prayers, intercession and thanksgiving be made for all people.*

I sat in the whirlpool staring at the clock. It read 6:15 AM on Saturday, February 12th, 2011, and I wasn't moving. I was thinking of all the things I was going to do for the day. All the things I did every Saturday, usually not the most productive day of my week, as far as doing a few things at home. I enjoyed starting the day off relaxing and enjoying some peace and quiet. A long workout followed by a little R & R in the whirlpool. This winter was getting long, lots and lots of snow and several of my son, Brenon's basketball tourneys. My daughter, Kippen was off at college and things around the house were different, big change with only one kid around. I really missed seeing her, but she was off growing up. It was always the same story, look forward to the weekend, and then in a flash it was gone. Also, spending time with my wife, Keri and getting a few projects done around the house. A few cold walks with my friend, Jeff and my little Westie dog, Jazzi, but winter was getting long.

Just like life, just flying by day by day, I used to think 30 was really old, now I was 50 and counting. Saturdays were usually filled with sports and house stuff, and Sunday we usually attended church at Hosanna in Lakeville, MN followed by a nice nap in the basement. Our Pastors at Hosanna always opened the weekend services with "God led us there."We discovered Hosanna back in the 90's. I was doing the Christian things every week with no real direction. I was very happily married to my wife Keri, sure we had the ups and downs of any marriage. But with life I was always wanting more, but not sure how to find it. Maybe plans to help others, always thinking of a mission trip after retirement. I knew I wanted to go help others at some point in later life. Maybe by the time I was retired at 65. That meant 15 more years and I would be ready to help others, so I thought. I always knew the Gospel and followed all the regular Christian plans. Bible study, church, and some weekly youth activities were part of my routine. I thought about all of this before that cold February morning. Not knowing that morning would change the path I was on and change the direction of my walk with God. I was teaching 6 to 8, 8th grade kids, including my son in our youth group program called Powerlife at Hosanna. You will read later a few stories of how God and those 8th grade boys transformed my life as far as the battle with temptations that I was supposed to be teaching them.

I was just coming off a tough 2010 year. Three good friends and another friend's nephew tragically lost their lives. On top of that my brother, Mike had just been diagnosed with colon cancer and had some pretty tough surgeries. That situation had taken a tough toll on my parents. Lots of crazy things were happening, and at the time it was tough on our entire family. All of the deaths were sad stories, everyone was asking the same question. Why so soon? Why Them? Why Now? Where was God in all of this? These thoughts kept running through my head? My closest loss was Jeff Barber, we had really gotten to know each other through our son's sports. His life ended suddenly in a parking lot at Lifetime Fitness due to heart failure. That was the one that got to me, he was just an awesome friend, and I can't wait to see him in Heaven. Can't wait to understand the reason God took him when He did. I just have to find out right away on that one. It is in the big plan and Jeff, like all of us, was a part of it. I really struggled with this for a long period of time.

Jeff was a great friend, everyone's great friend. He and I spent many hours watching our boys play sports and enjoying life. Jeff was one of those guys that only comes along once in a lifetime. But sadly his life ended almost as soon as our friendship began. He died April 29th of 2010. He died 15 minutes after leaving the exact whirlpool I was sitting in on the morning of February 12th of 2011; he was such a huge part of my life. Every time after his death that I went to the fitness center, he was in my thoughts. He still is every time I see something that reminds me of him. You see he died in the parking lot from a massive heart attack as he sat in his car ready to face another day. I always think of Jeff when I sit in the whirlpool at the club that day, and I think that is where he spent his final moments. I try to think what he was thinking minutes before he left this earth to be with his Maker. This is where the story really begins. Later I realized that both of these stories were connected in the circles we are all connected through each and every day.

The morning of Jeff's death I was milling around the house, trying to get work done, being distracted by a million different things. I always worked upstairs, because my cell phone worked best up there, mostly because we live out in the country. I was walking through our master bedroom and boom my cell phone was ringing. It said "Barber Home" on the digital read out and I answered, "Hey you big goof, what do you want?" The phone call I received was not from Jeff. It was from his wife Colleen. It still sends chills down by spine, Scott, "This isn't Jeff, it is Colleen. You need to sit down." I asked "Why?" and she said again, "Scott, you need to sit down." I knew before the words came out of her mouth. I said "Colleen, don't say it." I knew what happened before she said it; she never used that kind of voice with me. Then she said the words I will never forget, "Jeff is gone." I couldn't believe what she had said, and she went on to explain what had happened and about the heart attack he had suffered in the parking lot at Lifetime. Those words sent tears running down my face that didn't stop for days. The pit in my stomach was as deep as any hole I had ever felt. That pit I felt followed me everywhere for months, I just couldn't believe Jeff was gone. It was a really big shock to my heart and soul.

Sheila from Lifetime Fitness tried with all her will and strength to get Jeff back and breathing. We will be forever thankful to her for her compassion and courage. Sheila is a person, who I have now become friends with and have shared many stories between the two of us. The entire Lifetime Fitness staff ended up helping and even attended Jeff's first Charity Golf Tourney we had in his name. Jeff taught me two lessons, treat everyone with open arms, and also everybody is different. Treat them with love without judging them, and give people second chances and show them mercy. I am not saying I do this always; my flesh gets the best of me in many situations. Jeff reminded us that God made us all different. We are all very different for the wonderful purpose of enjoying life and loving one another. I still, to this day, say to people in crazy situations, "We are all different," a Jeff Barbers saying. That is what we printed on the T-Shirts for his golf tourney.

That ended up being the toughest day of my 50-year-old life. But I now realize "A Wonderful Life," Jeff's favorite movie, he got it. He was living the "there is no time like Heaven" life. Just try to find people in the community you can love and be loved by, live it out for the great moments. He lived his life with such happiness, and everyone knew him and his family. I am not saying he didn't ever complain, no one is perfect, but 95% of the time his walk was just love one another and order appetizers at every meal. Enjoy it, it goes fast! He was a man of faith, and that is all God asks. Romans 10:9, says, "confess with your lips and believe in your heart." Jeff believed. He also did anything to help people in his circle. He would drive and pick up friends at 2:00 AM who might not think it was too safe to drive. One of those guys helped plan the golf tourney and has become a good friend. Jeff was always there to help a family member or friend. We all have one of these type of people in our lives. A person that would drive 500 miles to help you change a tire. Jeff was that person, always looking out for others, and when you saw him you felt better about yourself. Jeff didn't run around judging others and tell them how they should live their lives, he just lived it by his actions. I miss Jeff every day and can't wait to see him in Heaven. We miss his ability to keep people together, but many of us who met him are carrying that on daily.

After that spring, the summer continued to tumble. Keri's friend Holly called one afternoon and told her that their friend Sheila had died. I stood and watched as all her high school friends just couldn't believe that their friend was gone in a flash, just like Jeff. Life is so precious. She died from a terrible car accident. She was like Jeff, she knew everyone. Standing in line at the funeral home, seeing the hurt on Shelia's husband, Jim was so hard to watch. But faith pulled him and his two daughters together. I haven't talked to Jim since, but I know our paths will cross again in the future. Sheila was a lot like Jeff, always smiling and asking how you were doing way before she wanted to talk about her own situation.

Wow, then there was Carter. My good friend Kelly's nephew was lost in a tragic accident. A 13-year-old boy with his entire life ahead of him, and he lived his life like Jeff. I never met Carter, but I sure feel I know him by seeing all the wonderful pictures and hearing the great stories. His life was stopped instantly by a rock while having fun at a park with some friends. Billions of tears, and billions of questions why, why so soon. It was all confusing to everyone involved why would God take such a young child? Why would God take a child so soon? Why would God take him now? My friend Kelly was the aunt of this wonderful boy, seeing the hurt in her eyes and the stories of unbearable sorrow will be with her sister every day of her life. But she too will be united with Carter, and I want to be there to see them embrace. I still think of Carter from time to time, and just how hard each and every day is for his family.

Then there was Dave. A man that lived his life like every day was his last. He, like Jeff, suffered a massive heart attack. Dave died on New Year's Day 2011. He was a good friend, and a very funny man. I worked with him in sales. We had actually attended a Search Ministries event together in November of 2010; he was very surprised by all the Vikings that were Christians. He was especially happy to see that Viking's star, Jared Allen, walked with the Lord. They didn't wear it on their shoulders, but you knew they were defenders of Christ.

He asked me several questions right after we heard Jared's testimony, and I know that triggered some deep thoughts about Dave's salvation, and his life.

It all hit me the summers of 2010 and 2011. They were tough years. I kept asking why in every situation. All the sudden deaths of Jeff, Sheila, Carter, and Dave made me think of how precious life is, and how fast it can end. I started to take an inventory of where I stood with God. I knew I was a Christian, but just didn't feel the Spirit working through me like I thought it should. I was good in areas of my life, but not so in some. I don't go around telling people how Christian I am, I just try to live my life the way Jeff did, being nice to one another. Of course, I don't live that way all the time, my temper gets the best me from time to time. But I am trying hard to change that part of my life. This all came to a point one day in the backyard. I was there doing some work, thinking about Jeff and the others, and I raised my hands in the air and asked God, why? Then I asked Him to show me why all these things happened. I asked Him to take care of my home and use me to show others what You teach me. That was it, this wasn't like me. It was crazy to think back of what I said that day; I believe that is the day it all started. That is the moment my life changed forever.

Back to that crazy morning sitting in the whirlpool, February 12th. As all these thoughts raced through my head, I was sitting in that whirlpool at Lifetime Fitness in Lakeville, Minnesota. I was staring at the clock at 6:05 AM, just another Saturday. I had my daily thoughts of Jeff and how much I missed his crazy laugh. I was thinking of my friend and his wife who were going through a terrible separation. A couple you would have never suspected to have problems. A couple that no one would have thought to split, but the world is evil and things happen. This was another situation where I was asking God, why? Ever since the first sin was cast, we will never know why, at least while we are here on earth. Just like the deaths that had spun through my life, no one could figure out why, we all have sin in our flesh. And sin does terrible things to families.

As I sat there relaxing, I didn't want to move. I kept thinking of my friend Mike and his situation. How could they be splitting up. They were the perfect couple. We had been in Bible study with him for over 15 years, and he had really helped build my foundation with God's word. I had been invited to a prayer intersession a few days earlier, through an email I received. I didn't know what prayer intercession was. Now it was early that morning and the intersession started in 25 minutes. There was no way I was going, not a chance. I had contacted Ben (he wrote the forward to this book) from my Bible study; and he decided not to attend either. We just didn't feel comfortable attending. Praying in tongues and praying through people was not our type of situation.

I looked at that clock on the wall, 6:07 now. No way, I don't attend those types of events. Maybe they will speak in tongues, I knew I wasn't ready for that. The email said God will speak through someone. I am a Christian, not a Christian that would be holy enough to have God move through me. No reason to go. Now, 6:08 and I was thinking of my friend, all the things he did for me over the years. He kept our men's Bible study together for 15 years, and was always there. He did the funeral service for both of my wife's grandparents, and he was there every time I needed a friend. So what was stopping me from going? 6:09, I was thinking of the prayer intercession and how these friends were going to ask God for direction. How God will work in my friends' lives to repair the hearts of the Christian's He loves. I was still not going to go, why would I attend something that made me uncomfortable and something that just wasn't supposed to happen?

6:10, the wave of emotion hit me like a ton of bricks. What are you doing? Where is your heart? Why wouldn't you go help your friend? Get up NOW! I stood up and walked as fast as I could across the slippery pool floor. The same floor, taking the same steps my friend Jeff had 10 months earlier. The same steps I think of every time I walk this floor. I was thinking about what was going through Jeff's mind as he spent his last minutes on earth. I showered and got dressed in record time. I got in my car and drove to Edina, where the meeting was being held. As I drove, God reminded me to have an open mind, and find out why my friends' marriage was so full of hurt. I was racing to the meeting, just a conference room in the middle of the Twin Cities, just a regular space where meetings are held each and every day. The room wasn't a place I wanted to be on that day. I pulled up to the office and I could see a light on, the room where this was all taking place. As I walked towards the office I could see the light, and the faces of the friends that were there to hear God speak. I was really nervous, not being comfortable in these situations.

I walked into the office of MA Peterson and home of Prayer Transformation Ministries (PTM) and this prayer meeting for my friend. It was dark out, and they had the lights on, but turned way down. I saw that they were all in this room, yet I knocked and asked for my friend Mike. As I stepped in the room, I quickly found a seat. When I first sat down I was thinking what am I doing? Why did I come here? Then I turned my attention to the man at the end of the table, he said "God will speak through one of us and we will get a clear understanding of what our friend needs to pray for and how we can all help." I sat there and realized something was about to happen. When I looked up I could see my friend Chris in the room too. He's one of my Christian friends that I respect. I hadn't seen him for months. I sat there staring straight ahead, watching the man at the end of the table. I realized that there were eight or nine people sitting around the room, sitting at a table all in deep thought and all of them were staring at the head of the intersession.

Then my friend Chris asked him a question, "who are you and where are you from and explain to me what we are doing here." He stopped and explained that he was Madan, a Christian missionary from India. He had attended many intercessions and he was ready to see God move through us. And he talked about how he learned how intersession and prayer can change the course of life. I started to get nervous and I wanted to speak up and explain to Mike that I was not even thinking of attending. Then, I explained to the group why I wasn't coming this morning but then I realized that something came over me as I was sitting in the whirlpool trying to come up with reasons not to attend. I explained what drew me there, and explained reasons why my friend in trouble was now in need of our help. I explained how he did the funeral service of both of my wife's grandparents in the past year. Also I realized that I was there for a reason and I looked at each one of them. Everyone was there to hear what God had to say. I was very emotional apologizing to my friend why I wasn't going to attend at first, but I was here now.

I still was at a point I didn't believe God was going to speak through anyone at that table. I actually started to panic and wonder how I would get a hold of my wife Keri if this kept going all day. I was also hungry and I was worried I would miss my son's basketball game later that day. That wasn't going to happen, I had never seen anything like this, these guys are nuts. There was real doubt in my mind, and then I started to think, let it happen for my friend!

As we all started to pray, I could feel the presence of God filling the room. But I still had doubts. Everyone continued to pray. Then, out of right field, it hit me, I could feel something moving through my arms, and they started to shake a little. I remember my prayer getting louder and more direct. Then my mind started to clear, like never before. I could start to see the image of Jesus in my open clear mind. I continued to pray. I could see a shadow of Jesus, right in my mind. Then as I started to pray, it happened. As I prayed I stopped thinking, the words were just pouring out. I remember small parts of my prayer, but not all of it. I later learned, Mark from PTM actually took notes of my prayers. Then I just stopped. As I raised my head Madan looked at me and said, "God has spoken, let's close in prayer." Wow, what had just happened I thought to myself? At first I thought maybe I fell asleep I've been known to do that in meetings and many times in school. I stood up and walked towards the door, as I got to the door I gave Mike a hug. Then I walked over to my friend Chris who I hadn't seen in months and gave him a hug. He looked me in the eye and said "Scott, that was awesome!," and he repeated again "that was just awesome! "

I shook Madan's hand, and thanked him and the host Mark from MA Peterson and PTM for having this prayer time. I walked out the door and walked towards my car. As I approached my car a man came up to me and introduced himself. He said that was one of the coolest things he'd ever seen. It was really sad to hear about my son's broken leg and told me he would pray for a speedy recovery. I explained to him, that it happened last summer and he was doing great.

Then he asked if my son was all right now, and I told him I was actually going to his basketball game later this afternoon. I opened the door to my car and sat down. I looked at the clock on the dashboard and it read 9:10 AM.

I could not believe that much time had passed and again I thought oh no, I fell asleep in there and I still didn't fully realize what had happened. Then as I started to drive I could feel inside my chest and body were completely cleared out. There was not one ounce of sin in my body. I felt like every ounce of sin I ever committed was completely washed away, and it was clean, completely clean.

As I drove I started to have some unexplained thoughts. This voice I couldn't hear, but I could feel was telling me to get a hold of Jay Subtad from Agua Viva, a small missions group started in our community by 4 men. The feeling to contact Jay wouldn't stop coming into my head. It wasn't like a regular thought, it was more like this overwhelming thought that wouldn't leave my mind. Is that how we learn when the Holy Spirit works in your life? As I continued to drive I could feel the Spirit still inside me, the Spirit that I could not explain. Then my cell phone rang, and when I picked it up and it was Chris on the line. He said, "Scott, why did you leave so quickly? I wanted to talk to you about what happened." He said that was one of the most awesome things he'd ever seen. I still didn't fully understand what he meant. I really felt great about helping my friend through his separation. I tried to focus on the real purpose of the intercession, and I continued to pray for my friend's marriage. Then Chris asked me for my old business partner Tom's phone number, and we agreed to get together sometime.

As I continued, reflecting on what I had prayed about that morning, and my thoughts started to come back of what I had prayed for my dear friend. I prayed for some type of direction for their separation and God's plan for his life. I remembered comparing their broken marriage to my son's broken leg and that healing could happen with prayer and intercession. Also I prayed about the 4 broken bones and 4 months, or 4 years of healing that could happen. As I continued to drive I could feel my entire body cleansed, I couldn't explain it. Now, I thought, how am I going to explain this to my wife Keri?

I pulled into the garage on that February 12th morning, and I walked into the kitchen. I remember telling Keri that I had just went through the most amazing experiences I had ever had and explained to her what it meant. As I told her she believed every word. She repeated some of it back, it sounded different that way, but it made sense. Then I continued to tell her how clean my body and soul felt, and not full of sin. I continued to tell her that Jay was on my mind, I couldn't stop thinking of him, almost like he was calling for help. This mission trip to Honduras was weighing on every thought I had, it was really overpowering me. I told Keri I've got to figure out how to contact Jay, I don't know why but I just need to get a hold of Jay. After visiting with Keri about the intercession, I proceeded to go on the computer and look for Jay's e-mail address. I searched every possibility and I couldn't find his e-mail address.

I thought about how I had met Jay, through our sons' lacrosse team roster. He had coached for a few years but I never really knew him. Then one day a group of 20 lacrosse parents were standing waiting for our kids to get their pictures taken. As we stood there rainclouds approached from the west, nothing threatening, just a little sprinkle. Everyone scattered to different sides of the field and Jay and I ended up under an overhang near the concession stand. We visited for a few minutes, and I asked him what he did for a living. He said he used to be a pilot for Delta Airlines. He told me how his life had turned to God and that now he planned mission trips to Honduras. He invited me to come to one of his dinners some time and learn more about the trips.

Well the fall passed, and I ran into him again at a fall football game, another "not by chance moment." I was just walking down the stairs, leaving a varsity football game. I found out later from Jay that he was asking God to have us run into each other if God wanted that to happen. I continued down and I was two sections over from him. The crowd in front of me started to back up so I ran over a few isles to find a quicker escape. Just as I made my way to a different aisle, there was Jay. We shook hands and talked about the game, then he invited me to an Agua Viva dinner the following Friday. As I walked away, I thought to myself, not a chance was I going to that dinner. Well, needless to say, the following Friday I attended the missions dinner by myself. I met some really nice people and thought that someday I would go on a missions trip. As I walked out of there, I thought I would go when I was retired, 15 years from then. Circle back to the morning of the intercession. I'm was trying to find Jay's e-mail when I realized what I was doing. Why was I trying to find Jay. This was about connections, this was about stories, this was about restoration to the connections of Christians. The circles, and the space God put there for all of us. I figured if I got a hold of somebody from Lacrosse, then they could find me Jay's e-mail address. As I sent the e-mail to my friend Jenny from Lacrosse, I prayed that somehow I would be connected to Jay.

On Monday morning, two days later, I got the e-mail from Jenny. She asked how I was doing and connected me with Jay. I sent an e-mail out right away to Jay, telling him I wasn't sure why but I needed to meet with him. So we set up a breakfast appointment for the following Thursday. Throughout that week, I talked with a few people from the prayer intercession, I was told I prayed for over 45 minutes straight. I couldn't believe that, I knew I'd prayed for maybe 10 or 15 minutes but I couldn't believe it was that long. Now I was completely drawn to learn to pray more. My friend told me about a prayer group at my church Hosanna. The prayer group called Prayer Force, started bright and early on Thursday mornings at 7 AM.

I couldn't wait to get there and when I arrived I felt very welcome. I just wanted to learn more about the power of prayer. I was so humbled by these people and all their different backgrounds meeting once a week to pray for the church, leaders, and friends in need. As I walked away from the prayer group, they felt like a family. Mike the leader, and my friend Andy, who invited me, made me feel so welcome. I also met one of the organizers Colleen; she was very nice also and made it a point to welcome me.

After the prayer meeting I went to meet Jay at a local restaurant for a quick breakfast to discuss what had happened the prior Saturday. I met Jay, shook his hand and we exchanged pleasantries. We ordered our breakfast and then I proceeded to tell him my story of intercession. Then I told him about standing in the kitchen with my wife and when I was driving home from Edina that God told me to find you; I didn't know why. I really wanted to just think I wasn't too weird; it was nice to just get that off my chest. I was just being told to meet with you. Jay couldn't believe his ears, and the tears started to stream down his cheek. He said he and his wife were praying for somebody to help them raise money for the next mission's trip. Agua Viva is a mission started by four men who wanted to make a difference in God's Kingdom and the restoration of

His Earth. Jay explained that normally through dinners and letter writing to friends and family, they raised enough money for most trips. But this one was different; this was a group of students from Bethel University located in Minneapolis. All the flights were paid for, but they needed money for extra supplies and the extra metal piping that was needed for a well they were building.

Jay proceeded to tell me, the trip was coming up short. He was in a bit of a panic with work, planning for this trip and providing for his family. I told him I was there to help. I would use creativity with my connections to relieve some his stress. Right then and there, we started thinking of ways to raise the money. And I told him again not to worry about it, that I was called to help him. Once again tears rolled down his cheeks, I know in his mind he was realizing how God answers prayers. At that point, I could feel the Spirit moving through both of us. He gave me the name of a person that could create coupons we could sell in the area around our church. Then I told him we should also meet with our missions director, Tim, because I knew we were going to need some people to help sell coupons. We left the breakfast energized and ready for battle.

After Jay and I met that day, it was on to a different prayer group. I was so fired up to be in God's presence anywhere I could find it. Prayer Transformation Ministries, the same place I just had my intercession was meeting at 11:30 AM. As I walked in to MA Peterson I could feel the presence of God again, just like the past Saturday. Once again I felt welcome in the group, like I belonged. I also made a connection with Colleen, a member of the Hosanna group that helped organize the group at PTM. As we all sat and found our places, Madan the prayer leader introduced himself. He quickly asked if I would share my story from the past Saturday. I was excited to share and I went through the wonderful story. That was when I really knew for the first time that what had happened was true and to the point. I was told by Madan that I spoke for over 45 minutes. My heart was filled with an unbelievable sense of joy. The Spirit of God was inside my entire body, speaking through me for over 45 minutes. It was a moment of joy and realization. The same Spirit that was on the cross, in the burning bush with Moses, and many more was inside of me explaining and guiding my friend in his time of separation from his wife. Now I really understood what the Spirit meant and how powerful God is in all of our lives.

Now look at the diagram on page 21 to see that first week and what the moment on February 12th meant for me, Scott Gulsvig, one guy in a small township in the middle of nowhere. Now God was using me to help expand His Kingdom. At this point I had no clue what he was about to show me. But I started to see how this was all connected.

The circle was small before I started to see the light God was offering me. We need to see the light of God in everything. Expanding our circle and connecting and creating other circles are how we create new christian culture and restoration. Culture is everywhere and in Gabe Lyons books "The Next Christians" he talks about creating culture with stories of people. These are the connecting circles. I went and saw Gabe Lyons at our church in the Spring of 2011. I signed up on a quick thought. It was on a Monday and I shouldn't have gone because of my work load that day. He talked about an organization that created T-shirts to combat teenagers that were cutting to triple X church trying to combat the pornographic industry. Gabe Lyons explained that they were creating culture for good in creating culture as they go. It just took a few days following the Spirit moving in me. I had a circle that had a Christian and Non-Christian influence.

My goal was to not worry about who was in the circle. Just how God was calling me to tell them my story and move in their lives. I started to hear God and move when He called. All of us don't need an intercession to figure this out; we just need to take the first step. Did I need more important people? No, just a great group of people that had an influence on my world. People have an inner drive to help, they want to help. They just don't know how. And if the circle stayed that size it would be just fine if that is what God was calling me to do. That is one point I learned about my journey; the circle can be as small as two people. God will use you in that regard. Trust me on this, it is not about the size of your circle, it is the calling God has put on your lives. My circles are getting bigger and bigger, I am listening to God each and every day. He is my guide, big or small.

This journey has been more about opening my eyes than anything. God does things all the time in our lives. We just have to see them. It is up to us to make our circles expand. We can sit back and just go to Church and go through the motions or we can choose to make connections. All for God's glory. It took getting out of the Whirlpool on Feb. 12th to see that! There have been 100's of people telling me how cool of a journey I am on. But if I would have sat there on that day and not listened to God, I would not be writing this book right now. I would have been just like everyone else. When did you miss your God moment? Only He knows. Now I never hesitate to witness or to step up with a faith idea. It is all God. Maybe my God and Spirit moment would have been when I was 18 or 30. I will never know. I just decided to get up and listen to the calling on February 12, 2011. I know I was a Christian at the time. I accepted God into my heart many times in youth church activities, but the time I remember it really sticking was in my junior year of college in 1983. Active in many things at church, I was on the sidelines, just an equipment guy. Not even close to the fields. That is one of the illustrations I use all the time, who gets a ring when a team wins the Super Bowl? It really helps bring home my point. Do the people that play just get them? This is from an article I found from AP writer Rachel Cohen :

When the Pittsburgh Steelers won the Super Bowl last year, every single one of their full-time employees got a ring — but they didn't necessarily receive the same gaudy ones as stars like Ben Roethlisberger. Players, coaches, football operations staff and other top-level employees got a ring that weighed 3.7 ounces and included 63 diamonds totaling 3.61 carats. The rings were cast in 14-karat yellow gold with black antique backgrounds. Female employees received a smaller version because the full-size ring would have been too big for them to wear.

Lower-level employees received a ring with less gold and fewer diamonds, since buying the full-size ring for the entire organization would be prohibitively expensive. The NFL pays for up to 150 rings at $5,000 apiece, with the club picking up the rest of the cost.

This is the way I like to think of my life before I stepped out of the whirlpool. I was on the team in the back office, but I really wasn't on the field. As you look at the following illustration, it shows you can either be on the field or off the field. I think people get too hung up worrying about doing huge things. I recently saw Joel Manby speak at our church. He repeated a great line that he had heard. "Do for one what you wish you could do for everyone." I absolutely love that quote, because most of us stress that we're not doing enough for others. Don't look at it that way, if you're on the sidelines and you want to get on the field, think of one person you can help. It could be somebody in a nursing home, it could be someone in your neighborhood, or it could just be leading a small group of youths at church. That is stepping back on the field, that is causing circles to connect and being in the community. That is exactly what stepping on the field is, it doesn't have to be writing a book or doing something that you think isn't making a difference. Just do as Joel said, do something for one person. That is stepping on the field. That is becoming part of the team. That is helping restore and make this world a better place.

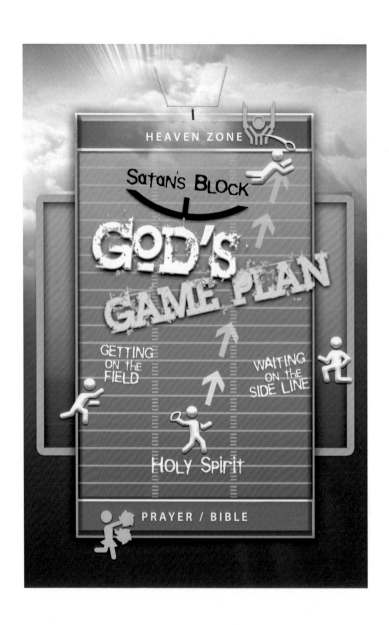

Here is my point, before I jumped out of that whirlpool on that cold winter morning, I was on the team. I wasn't on the field; I was as involved as I could have been without stepping on that field. I was part of the team, God's team and was getting closer to Him at a snail's pace. I went from a 2 mph wind to a tornado. My life turned upside down after that day of the intercession. I look back and I am 100% sure that if I would have died before February 12, 2011 I would have gone to Heaven. You might be on the team too, just waiting for God to call you. Just be ready, He is sneaky fast when He wants you to be in the game. He usually grabs you when you don't even have your uniform clean and ready. This is where I really think the rubber hits the road. I been sitting in church every week for years, hearing how we can be more involved, and how I said I would get more involved as I got older especially when I was retired. God has called me on the field now, to write this book and make the gospel simple. I've always been part of His team, not on the field. And I think one of the goals for me in this endeavor is to bring Heaven down to earth. Just like the title says "There's No Time Like Heaven" I truly believe, through one believer in one follower at a time, we can make earth as it is in Heaven. Just like the Lord's prayer says, on the field or off the field, we can still make a difference.

I think the main thing we need to do, is figure out what gift we have, where we can make a difference. I get so charged up by hearing stories time and time again of people that use their gifts for God's glory. Their gifts to just make a difference, one story at a time these kids can be lifted up and make earth as it is in Heaven. One of my goals is to bring stories to life in a future book. Every day I hear stories on the radio, on TV, on the Internet, in church, or even the local coffee shop. These stories will really make the difference, stories of people just stepping out, getting on that field, doing it for God's glory.

That's the big difference, when you change it from being about you to being about God there is glorification in that and that's where I think you can make a difference. We are all in this together; we have to use each other's talents to change this place called Earth for the good. I started listening to books on tape, and you will see I have included books as you watch my circle grow. I think in the Lords prayer when we pray, "on earth as it is in Heaven," we need to create a place that God wants us to have on earth. Gabe Lyons and his restoration ideas have really inspired me to find ways to aid in restoration. The Bible is the book I have always read; it has been a great inspiration. Now, I just don't read it I meditate on every word. I do have a weakness for remembering stories and verses. That is something I have to learn to do, and should be a goal of ours.

I really haven't changed a ton personally, I still treat people the same way as I did, and I surely don't go around telling people all the things that I see being done each day. I just try to stay humble and let people see who I am by my actions. Then you see yourself in more circles, don't try to create ones that have no meaning, let God lead you to the ones that matter. It's like when you release a hand full of balloons. Some go straight up, and come right back down. Some can float all the way around the world. Let your heart lead you, sit at a different table in class, talk to someone you haven't talked to in years. Try a different path home. Call an old friend. Ask a neighbor to coffee. Make your circles count for God's glory. Be ready to help when needed. Pray so that the end result is for Him. I pray every day for help to find the words for this book. This book is living proof that we all have this in our lives if we just ask for the help from the Holy Spirit. You don't need to be a pastor, a scholar, or a theologian. You Just Need to ASK! And for me, I am doing it for God's glory. NOTHING ELSE!

And it's really fun!

CHAPTER 2

Getting Involved
The Buckets

Matthew 7:3 - "Why do you look at the speck of sawdust in your brother's eye and pay no attention to the plank in your own eye"

I have always lived my life in sections; I have the same personality but act differently in different situations. I am trying to be more consistent in all areas of my life, and challenging myself in a number of different areas. I still am my same goofy self with family, church, and friends. I still love to have a ton of fun in all those areas, but sometimes I just wish I could be the same in all those areas. I call these "The Buckets", the different areas in our lives. I don't think we can have complete peace with ourselves and consistent values in all the areas of our walks until we figure all these areas out. You see how Heaven really was on earth, and it still can be. If you look at the way Heaven is moving away from earth, it is the real truth of how we all look at ourselves and we are not reaching out to others for restoration. Heaven on Earth! Heaven is on Earth, it is here in all the moments we live when we do the right things. NOT the things just to satisfy us, but the ones that make this a better place. I just wish we could all be consistent all the time, but we all know it is not possible living in the flesh. Some Christians react and defend themselves from being involved. Religion is not about being involved, it isn't about how much time you spend or how involved you are, God loves us all just the same no matter how much time we spend. Romans explains how Paul taught that involvement doesn't matter as much as the heart is connected to God.

So we can't and shouldn't judge others for how much time they spend in community learning about God and the Spirit. That is a big bucket for me, judging is a real area I have to work on. I judge them all: friends, family, coaches, and Christians. And sometimes youth athletes, how low can I go right? Before February 12th and the second I stepped out of the whirlpool, I was one of those people that believed God would reward me daily for my time I devoted to Him. It was like a check list, to show others all the stuff I do to get acceptance from other Christians. That is not how it works, works are just works whether they are Spirit-induced or not. We don't get to Heaven by works, not one person on this earth will ever enter the Heavenly gates by works. The Grace of asking God into our hearts is the only way to enter Heaven that is spelled out throughout the Bible. The amount of stuff we do doesn't matter to God, what matters is our heart and what we are doing to expand His Kingdom. That is all it is, each one of these stories expands His Kingdom. It's all about Grace, and believing God exists and working towards Him from that point.

I really truly think we cannot fix this place we call earth until we decide that we have to fix our temples or our own kingdoms. Those temples are our bodies, full of these buckets that never seem to make sense until we examine each one of them. We have to look deep inside ourselves before we can start helping others. Along the way we can love everyone, just as Jesus wants us to, but we can't change people if we haven't changed ourselves. That is what cracks me up most about this mess we find ourselves in, no one admits they have any problems. That's fine, not judging here but it's just crazy how people like me try to change others and I have so much changing to do myself. Just crazy how it all works, it would be like a surgeon who hasn't finished the heart section in college operating on a heart. You have to know how to do the operation before you can operate.

God loves leaders and missionaries, Mother Teresa, Billy Graham, or one of us just having coffee with a buddy. It doesn't matter God loves us all equally. We are all going to spend eternity in Heaven through the sacrifice He made on the cross. Nothing else, it is a free gift, not a gift we have to pay a price for by doing good works. When you realize that it is not a challenge to prove how many good works you can do, it frees you to do it for God's Glory and his Glory only! That is when the light bulb goes off and you start to grow by faith and not by a check sheet of how much time you spend with God. But once we realize that, we can start to peel off all the layers this world has put on us, and get back to the core of just being honest and truthful each and every day. Then go help others, become the surgeon with the gift you have, and know that gift is to help others.

This is when you start to realize the freedom of living by the Spirit and not living by trying to please God—my biggest struggle, still! Each day I think what I do will affect how He treats me. Read the book of Job and that will make you see it differently. I have had this exchange happen in my life and I have seen Heaven on Earth several times, by trusting that He will show me these things that I was missing. The exchanged gospel that you will start to tell will be your stories. I am still an infant in the scheme of the total picture of living a true Spirit-filled life. These are baby steps; they don't happen all at once. They slowly start to build on each other. Matthew, Mark, Luke, and John, and the most important, your Stories. Yes, there aren't 4 Gospels, there are 5. Our stories are what get people off there duffs and become more involved. The rewards are immeasurable, the stories never end. I have "One A Days", daily miracles that I see all the time. God connecting the dots, and the circles to restore Heaven on Earth, this stuff is real.

I think baby steps are the most important thing, in Matthew 9:9 it is so simple it's scary. But the more you learn, the more it all makes sense. I am not going to lie to you and say it isn't easy sometimes, but the tough times are when you learn. It's when your radar is on full go, that's when it really soaks into your heart and soul. When Jesus passed through there He saw people that wanted to follow Him. He called out to Matthew, sitting in the tax office and He told him to follow Me. Matthew rose and followed Him. This is where I wonder why people make it so complicated to follow Jesus. That's all it says Matthew rose up and followed Jesus. It doesn't say that Matthew got on his knees, asked for forgiveness and totally resurrection of life. It just says that he stopped and followed Jesus. That is so important when you are explaining to others what it is like to follow Jesus. Romans 10:9. Just make the opening for the Holy Spirit to enter, open the gate. I know people will disagree with me on this one, and I'm not trying to be any different or create my own agenda. I am quoting straight out of the Bible, it says Matthew got up and followed Jesus. I've heard many stories of Christians that are witnessing to others and tell them to completely change their life in order to follow Jesus. That's not what Matthew 9:9 says. It says Matthew got up and followed Jesus. It's not to say that

Matthew didn't change while he was following Jesus, it just says that he followed Him.

Can you imagine what those first few days were like for Matthew following Him: the miracles he saw, all the people he spoke to, the conversations he had, the teachings. That is what must have been a true miracle for Matthew. Right after Matthew 9:9, Jesus went directly to Matthew's house for dinner. Those who went to dinner with people like that, weren't even close to being Christians. They were sinners and tax collectors. The people would stay away from them because they were such sinners. But Jesus got Matthew in there to tell stories. Matthew was being touched by Jesus. That's why Matthew is my favorite gospel. This part of the story just pulls out exactly how we should be living our lives. When I look at my story, I am so similar to Matthew. Throughout my high school and college years I was following Jesus but I hadn't committed to Jesus yet. Then towards college I committed to Jesus, through baby steps, one day at a time. And then I went through a period from about 23 to 50-years-old when I learned intercession was in the power of the Holy Spirit. I didn't waste that time, I learned throughout that time. But I truly believe it wasn't my choice, I was following Jesus and learning from Him. Like I said in the first chapter, I wasn't on the field to play but I was still on the team. What is so awesome about Jesus is He wants us on the team, and He wants us to follow Him. But He doesn't judge us, and cut us down when we aren't one hundred percent committed to Him.

That's why the stories are really worth it. I love hearing stories about people who have fallen over and over but God still pours His mercy down on them. I kind of did it backwards, now I'm starting to really learn about the people in the Bible. And the more I learn the more I realize everyone, yes I mean everyone, lives in the flesh. We all fall, but God will constantly show mercy toward us. Take time and learn about David and the trials and some of the things he went though. God always showed His mercy towards David, and I can't wait to spend time under the mango tree hearing David tell his stories. People want to hear stories, especially from people they trust. 71% of Christians lead there by a personal relationship with a friend or family member. They are burned out on the messages from some of the religious connections they have trusted in the past. Now they are turning to someone who lives it out 24/7. They see the joy in their hearts and they want that in their lives. Witnessing is about planting seeds so when people do make the choice to trust God, they have the full understanding of the entire picture.

Real stories are what people want; they also want to know how it began and how it is going to end. Gabe Lyons talks about it in his books. People are obsessed with that, and they go by the thousands to see movies like Independence Day and 2012. Everyone wants to know how and when they are going to die. A lot of plots have to do with how our soul and our dreams affect our lives. That is part of the involvement; we get those answers from the true journey of our lives, not from Hollywood.

Just like when I discovered Exodus when I was studying the word a few weeks ago. I had seen the story of the parting of the Red Sea hundreds of times. Studying the same story and passages in my community I realized the importance of the Red Sea crossing. It tells us that we have an escape with Jesus, when we are down and out we just look to Him and He will provide a way out. I was reading about the Red Sea and the Miracle of the crossing around the 10th anniversary of 9/11. I think some of those people during 9/11 looked towards Jesus and escaped to the eternal life that awaited each of them. He will have a path open for us to walk through, protecting us all along the way.

Just like when Moses' back was against the wall. Moses stood at the base of the Red Sea as the Egyptians descended on the millions of Israelites. The Israelites doubted Moses and said, "Now What Moses"? He told them to believe and it will be, trust the Lord our God. They still doubted at that point, they all wanted to go back to slavery. Just like when we doubt God will get us out of a bad or tough situation.

Moses told them to trust in the Lord, and they still didn't believe. Then Moses lifted his staff and parted the sea. He trusted God with getting them out of a tough situation, and it is one of the most powerful stories in the Bible. We have to trust God, and also learn more stories about how others have put complete faith in Him in a number of situations. Just like the stories of the Bible, we will find story after story of people in community trusting God for their needs.

That is a huge reason to be involved in community, to see others and get the support of how they trust God in different situations. I also learn more when I am in community; it is nice to see how others look at different stories from the Bible, and how they relate to them in their own lives. Life is really about just that, being in community, learning in community, and praying for one another in community.

When I came back from Honduras, I ended up with an infection in my leg from some bug bite. I had the ability to send out text messages and emails from my hospital bed. Within 15 minutes of sending the messages, 30 to 50 people were praying for me and my recovery. I almost felt embarrassed by the response. I felt so loved. That is what community is all about; God and the love of one another supporting our daily lives. To me that is "Earth as it is in Heaven". That is all we will feel in Heaven, without the embarrassment.

I truly believe with all my heart, this is the way we will restore this messed up greedy world, through lifting each other up and learning from the trials and live's of others. This is the life that I just love right now—so many of us just living through the word and through prayer. Intercessory prayer that truly is for God's glory. I just don't think you can do this on your own, period! That is the belief I have come to. We need to be involved and constantly build each other up, in community.

Consistent buckets build trust in your circles and also help make restoration possible. This should be every Christian's goal—to live in the same bucket, not one bucket for one circle, and another bucket for another circle. The circles make more sense with the same person connecting with the other circles.

If one circle is a hypocrite and the other circle is a person that lives a life of lies. There is no way the circles can interact as the circles get smaller and smaller closer towards God. Living in a community of people that all have one goal of making this world a better place is something we learn when we live in community. I am trying to build my community of friends and support through being more consistent in each area of my life. I like what U2 singer Bono says, "Who knows who you are? So just be yourself."

This is NOT easy; I only know a handful of people that actually live the same in all areas of their lives. Being consistent isn't easy; we are constantly trying to live up to others expectations. We are constantly trying to get ahead and try to impress others. The older I get the more I start to realize it is about others, not me. I try to keep others in my sights, to see what I can do for each of them. Worlds can crash together when you live a life like this, similar to George on the show Seinfeld. He was always worrying about his worlds colliding. There is also several books on trying to make your life more consistent, being the same person at the workplace as you are in church. We need to try being the same person with friends and at church. This is the one area I think most of us struggle with—trying to be a consistent person all of the time.

35

Rate each bucket from 1 to 10, (10 being most involved) based on how you live in each group. Please be honest. When you look at these areas of your life you will see how inconsistent you are in these different buckets. I am a 4 with my high school friends and a 10 in my Thursday morning prayer group. Now how can I live in community and be the same person across the board. I am trying to improve in each area. Make more buckets if you like, or change the areas you think are most important to you. This has been just as important to me as the planting seeds discussed in chapter 6. I have really been trying to get my home bucket more consistent with how I am supposed to live according to being a spiritual leader.

Living in community is great. But I am struggling to be the same in all areas of my life. When you make a change spiritually, like I did, you find out the people close to you are the hardest to convince you have changed. I look at my family; they have seen my temper and my foul language at times. I still overreact way too much to situations, especially with the kids, but that is my flesh speaking out and not the Spirit inside me. I want to get to a 24/7 exchanged life and it is very difficult to get to that point. We can all strive towards it, taking baby steps one inch at a time. How can we restore the mission if we don't have the mission turned on 24/7? We can still have fun and enjoy life, but we can do it always seeking Him in all situations. We also don't have to live in community with our trusted friends all the time. As it says in Hebrews 12, we need to live outside the gate. Go and be with the poor, the weak, and the ones that are suffering. It says that is where we will find Jesus. We also need to be intentional about spending time with family and friends.

The first time I saw a real 24/7 intentional life was when I went on a mission trip to Honduras. It was right in front of me. Living intentional and being with 8 others that had the same goal of being focused on getting water to the poor, but better yet delivering living water to their hearts. That was what I started to feel about 2 days into the trip. I started to focus on the fact that they might not hear the gospel for years. So, that is when I started to focus on bringing the stories to them. Getting involved is not easy and it is a choice to be learning and growing in your faith. What would this world look like if everyone spent the same amount of time in community praying and learning as they spent watching TV. The average American spends 14.6 hours a week watching TV. If you spend 11 hours a week in prayer and learning you will be so connected with the Spirit of Christ it will blow your socks off. 11 hours is exactly 10% of your waking time, if you exchange TV time with community time I guarantee you will understand what this all means. I am not saying I do that, just saying how cool that would be to have that in our lives. You will see what it is like to get to the edge of Heaven. There have been many times that I have seen the Glory of Christ come down in situations. When this happens you will know it and you will see the Glory of God on earth. This is the Heaven on earth we can all experience. You cannot do this without praying and clearing out your mind of all evil distractions. This is when we see the Glory of God bring Heaven on earth. I believe this is the ONLY way we will ever restore this earth to what God wants for us, we are not going to do it by pushing Jesus out of our lives and world.

I also imagine the entire world on an old style scale. A scale that has two sides. Imagine a balance of each side of your life. I see each day as either Heaven on Earth, or Hell on Earth. I know that sounds harsh, but if you look at each day like that, you can ward off the evil spirits that are attacking us each minute. There are so many distractions and things that keep us from focusing on Christ it is amazing. Just the everyday lives we live, that is enough to keep our focus on things that have no bearing on how we live the everyday walk. This life is hard; I do a ton of comparing to others. Especially those that I met in Honduras, they were working all the time to keep their families protected. I know we do the same, but we don't need to do it with cell phones and video to keep us distracted. I think that is the area that is really being wedged into our lives, and the next generation's lives. I am sometimes sitting in prayer and worship times where people have their cell phones on and sitting on top of their Bibles. When I see that, I know that is a perfect illustration of what is running our lives.

Life is all about balance, all I know is the more I have Christ in my life the more balanced I feel. Life is really about finding Heaven on earth. Seek it out; I know it is there. I have seen it. See the Glory of God in everything you do, good or bad. But it is a way to realize that He does things to help us see His Glory. Hopefully you will begin to see that the more involved you become. I don't think we should ever go around telling people we are Christians. I think that will be shown to people by our actions and how we live our lives. We talk about getting involved, anywhere, anytime. But it doesn't have to be 24/7, or perfect, but it does have to be done with an open heart. You have to believe the Holy Spirit will be constantly looking to use you, and use your gifts to fulfill His plan. We all have gifts, and we all have ways we can make this world a better place. We need to start from the inside out.

The bucket I am working the most on is my marriage bucket. I struggle with some of the fleshly things that I have never been able to crack. The number one thing I struggle with is my temper. I am like a boiling pot, I can go for weeks and then all the sudden, ba-boom. You don't want to be around when that goes off. It's like an atomic explosion. My poor wife and kids are always on the other end of it, and man it is easy to do when you get used to it. Then I really started to look at this bucket. This is the one that I really needed to fix the most. I never put my wife before me, and I know I didn't appreciate her as much as I should have. So I started to pray for this bucket, especially the temper part. I started to first work on just not leaving after a big fight. That was so hard, I couldn't believe how hard that was, every part of me wanted to run away from the conflict.

One Saturday afternoon, I was working around the house—doing what I wanted to do. Then Keri had a project she wanted me to help her with. Most of the time if I have an agenda I don't want to help anyone, especially my wife. So I ended up throwing a big fit and we got in an argument over something dumb. I yelled at her and stormed out of the house. I got in my car, sat there and prayed. I felt something pulling me back into the house. The minute I walked back into the house my daughter Kippen was standing in the kitchen. Her first words were, "What are you doing here, I thought you had a fit and left?" Wow, my own kid had seen me do this over and over and she saw the pattern of the past. But wait, the pattern had changed. I stepped into a new place of not leaving and my daughters comment assured me that I was trying to change. To me that was a huge breakthrough, and I see that moment as the day I started to let God change me. I really started to pay attention to my patterns, and how they just took over situations.

The last 6 months I have fallen back in the hole and let my fleshly body take over. Keri and I got into a big fight over how we were disciplining our son, Brenon. I ended up shutting her out for almost 3 days. What a dork I can be, just a royal dork.

I am realizing I have many faults, the biggest is the temper I have towards Keri when things don't go my way. It just gets plain silly how I react to situations. I have been really working to make this better, but not by myself this time, no way.

I have been praying that God would show me how to change. Recently we both had a situation where we had a disagreement with some parents. Heated words were exchanged. The situation really hurt both of us, but it was really hurting Keri. She had a sleepless night, then the next morning we went to my daughter's college for a concert and I prayed during the 4-hour drive. I asked God to show me how this situation would reveal to me why this even happened. I truly think God is always showing us something in all situations, if we look for it. But what was God trying to show me in all this? All things happen for God's glory, I firmly believe that and I was trying to see what He was showing me.

We greeted our daughter and had a wonderful lunch with her and my mother-in-law. Later that afternoon we attended her concert. It was sold out so we arrived early. As my wife and I were sitting there 20 minutes before it started, I began thinking about what had happened and how bummed Keri was over the situation. Then the light bulb went off, right there in an auditorium on a little campus in northwest Iowa, God revealed it to me. I asked her when I yell at her and throw my fits does it hurt worse than the confrontation we had the night before. I knew the answer before I asked it. "Of course, it does," she said. That was the moment I was praying for. I felt hurt and at that very moment I knew I was being healed.

In Romans it talks about not being conformed by the patterns of this world, but have your mind transformed through Jesus and the Holy Spirit. Now I finally realized the hurt I put her through all these years. I was bummed when this entire situation unfolded, now I was thanking God for it. Truly thanking Him for showing me through the valley of how His love works After 28 years of marriage the light bulb went off. I know I won't be perfect in the future, but I can honestly tell you, I am trying as hard as I can

Sure, there will be times when lack of sleep and worldly stress take over, but I know I will react differently and that is what I thank God for each day. Marriage is so holy, it has to have the mixture of God's love to survive. I know that had protected our marriage. So many times it would have been super easy to walk away, but we have fought through all the valleys and really seen the healing that can happen. I won't do it on my own like in the past. I need to have God in the center and always trust that the patterns will be changed.

This bucket has started to fill up just in the recent weeks. Keri and I are now more of a united front with our teenage son and finding ways to solve problems together. I stopped using "little white lies" to avoid conflict. Now the listening card is a tough one. But wait! Noah built an ark with no electricity and Moses parted the Red Sea with a piece of wood, so I know miracles can happen. I am working on that one. But seriously, I know that if I keep praying I know God will change my patterns in this world.

These buckets are in all of our lives. Create your own buckets. Pray each day they will improve, it won't be easy. Other buckets were also affected by recent events in my life. Later in the book I explain the salvation, sanctification, and service process. Sanctification is a hard process, it is the process of your spirit being tested and processed. Just like any processing, it's going to be grounded and squeezed, but the final product will be inspected and approved by only One! So it takes time, it might take a lifetime, but it will be worth all the trials that aide on that processing. One important note, you have to be connected to God's word during this time. Without that you won't have an anchor to hold on to and you could drift off to nowhere land.

The coolest part is that Noah didn't have a rudder, an oar, or a compass. He just trusted God was leading him to the shore. That was by far the hardest part; the letting go of the flesh and letting Him guide the ship. My giant ship is turning with a ton of resistance, but it's so rewarding on the other side of each situation. The best part is to take one situation and watch the ripples go out in hundreds of directions. Just follow one of those and see God in all of them. It's just crazy, one of these might affect 5 buckets. Try it, you'll like it. I could tell you 5 buckets were affected in the parent conflict Keri and I had, but I would have never seen that years ago. I truly believe I was going through the process then, I just wasn't looking for anything other than myself.

So check out these buckets, score yourself and get out of the way. Get as far out of the way as you can. Let the Holy Spirit grab the rudder and see where you go. It's going to get stormy and you will get scared, but trust and faith is part of the process.

CHAPTER 3   Wary of Wolves
In Sheep's Clothing

Matthew 7:15 - *"Beware of false prophets who come disguised as harmless sheep but are really vicious wolves."*

    Madan is a true missionary for God. He travels to India four to six times a year training leaders and sharing the Gospel. His heart is for the Dalits to learn the hope that they have never had. Madan, told a great story at prayer group recently. The story is about Eskimos and how they sometimes capture wolves. These Eskimos, their animals and the livestock that they own are constantly being attacked by wolves. So one of the ways they combat the wolves, to end their violent behavior is to do the following. They take a very sharp knife and layer it with blood, they let layer after layer dry on the knife. They take the knife and stick it in the ground or in the snow with the blade up, and just leave it for the wolves. The smell of the blood attracts the wolves like a dead animal would bring them in. As they approach the knife, the smell brings them closer. The wolf can't wait to get his mouth on the blood he smells. Then the wolf will lick the knife until the blood is gone. As he licks the knife it cuts his tongue, and the wolf starts cutting and numbing his own tongue. He tastes his own blood and starts to lick even more, which causes more cuts so severe it ends up killing itself.

Think of that in our own lives, when a sin starts to eat at our very core, it destroys us from the inside out. I think that is why we need to always look from the inside out, and start each day cleaning the garbage that has eaten our insides. I really truly think that this is the only way to start your day. It gets you centered, and cleans your mind, soul, and body. If you are always in a rush in the morning, pray yourself clean in the shower or on your commute to work. That is what we need to do every day. Our bodies are temples and we need to treat them like they are a true temple of God. Not only keep them physically fit, but spiritually fit too.

There are wolves in sheep's clothing everywhere, just waiting for you to take a lick and start the process of destroying your insides. The key is to stay away from the temptation that destroys your faith and life and restore yourself from the sin. That's why it's so important to start your day off with a devotion and the cleansing of your heart. The following is an illustration of the Wolf and how he attacks us each and every day. Look at the illustration and beware of the daily temptation.

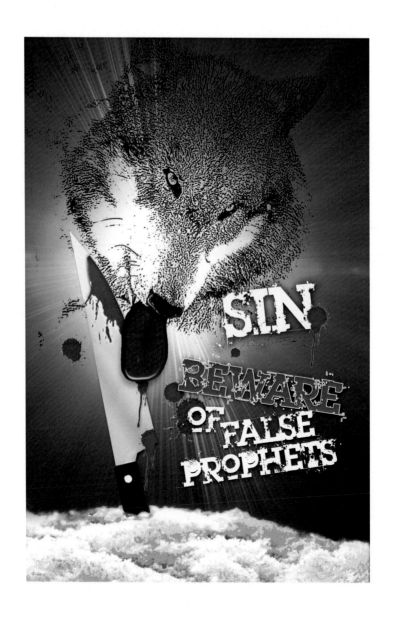

When I look at the sin in our lives; it is like the blood on the blade just layers and layers that build up and makes us numb. I have been trapped in these sins over and over in my life, and the sins we commit without even realizing it are the worst. I think that is why we need to be continually open to reading the Bible and learning more how others handle the different situations. Yes, sins becomes habits, it is us realizing the habit, and the sin gets so deep we want it more and it finally tastes so good we cannot break through it. I remember when my Dad smoked 1 to 2 packs of cigarettes a day, now he can't stand the smell of smoke. The habits of sinful cycles are the hardest thing to break. I think the only true way is to break through is to see how our sins affect others.

Andy Stanley says "Sin habits are making us realize that we don't trust God anymore." And as Andy states there is a difference between mistakes and sin. This is where we have to start, also making sure we seek to be around people to help us break away from the sin that is making us break away from God. One of the biggest parts of my walk is to be prepared for the enemy each day, and I know I have my guard up, staying in prayer and asking for protection. The attacks come non-stop in our lives; we just need to end up without the knife destroying our tongue and any part of the rest of our lives.

Pastor Andy Stanley also talks about Matthew 4 where it says that we have responsibility to fight off the sin, and pray that the Holy Spirit will help us in the battle field. In Matthew it explains how we need to fight the battle every day. My anger was one of the hardest things for me to tackle. I would be holding things in and letting them build up until the smallest thing would trigger me to get upset with my wife or kids. I am still trying to tackle it. The flesh just takes over in those moments. I don't even realize how or why I am getting mad.

That is where we need to really reach down and know that we can trust to have the Holy Spirit help us through the battle on the battle field. I know we are never going to be perfect and we are going to make mistakes. Again mistakes are mistakes, but when we know we are going to commit a sin, when we see it coming, those are the type of sins we can avoid.

That is where the understanding of the compartments or the buckets comes into our lives. We have to slowly learn to change and use the power of the Holy Spirit to help us. One area I know that has helped me change is just being more open to praying and telling others about my sins. Having an accountability partner is a great first step. Just being able to admit your sins and to talk them out is a great start. In one point in my life I would occasionally look at things on my computer and the World Wide Web. I knew I shouldn't be looking at them, and yet I would do it. This wasn't fair to my wife or others that I was ignoring to get the stupid excitement from the time I was on there. At the time I was leading a group of boys in a small group at our youth program called Powerlife. This all came to a head one night when we were attending a retreat in northern Minnesota. Things got pretty personal as the speaker was talking about the dangers of the internet. He was telling these 7th grade boys how it can become addicting and ruin lives and relationships.

I sat there and listened to the message, and just kept my thoughts and my secret habit to myself. We had also heard a message weeks before from a mission called xxx church. Yes, that is correct. www.xxxchurch.com a site to help people be released from online addiction. These were a few guys that are on a mission to stop online pornography in the church and outside the church. They had huge crazy statistics on how Christians have one of the worst problems in this area. One of the main problems was that they tried to be so good in the public eye, but when they were alone it overtook them. I never thought that I had a problem, just felt ashamed to talk about it. At the retreat, the leader speaking that night really drove it home. After his talk we met as a group in the back of the church. My boys were ashamed to even begin a conversation. My son was there to, so it made it really uncomfortable for me.

We started to discuss as a group, questions to get them thinking about the topic. Then it happened, one of the boys point blank asked me if I have ever looked at nasty things on the computer. At first I was shocked he would ask, but we were really leaning in on the topic and why not. I first paused and asked the Holy Spirit to reveal an answer for the boys. I wasn't at first going to tell them the truth. I was going to be like one of those Christians that would fake an answer and hide form the truth. Then after I asked the Holy Spirit I felt this feeling I should tell the truth. With my son sitting 3 feet from me I told the boys, "Yes, I have and it is wrong." I explained that I have looked at things online that were wrong and that I need to deal with it and pray about my situation. Wow, at that point some of the boys let out their guilt of some of the things they had looked at while they were on their parent's computer. One boy admitted he did it at least once a day. Another talked about how he had looked at some pictures he shouldn't have. It was an awesome night, and we prayed for each one of us to stop the cycle of sin.

As the year went on we approached the topic openly and had good discussions around the nasty things the world pulls us in to. I realized that being honest was the only way to answer these boys questions. It really formed a wall of trust around us, not a wall of lies between us. Just like the wolf, people are being sucked into the chains of sin from starting at just a small step.

I look at my own life and see how the access to these things is just getting worse each day. We can find this stuff in seconds today. I told my kids that night about my childhood and that we didn't have access to what they do today. My friend Joe and I did a paper route after school. When we were done we would go up in Joe's garage and we would look at some magazines of his. It was our form of internet back in the 70's. But with these we had to work hard to get our paper route done early in order to go and take a look.

I explained to my boys in the group that this wasn't right. But I did explain that it took hours to get to that point. Joe and I would do the paper route in record time just so we can go up in Joe's garage attic and look at some of these magazines. What is available today is different. Now kids can access pornography anywhere at any time! Some parents say they put parental controls on it, and that is great. But seriously, it's everywhere. On YouTube you can find just about anything. Sin is everywhere, just like the Wolf. Now they can click on a button, anywhere at any time. These kids can access it 24/7. The temptation is so much greater as our society is completely run by sex, because that is what sells. Most of the commercials are run with tons of images. The way we look and act is just very harmful.

That means we have to constantly be prepared, knowing that we will be tempted all the time. It is continually coming at us from all directions, so our guard just has to be up. We just need to be prepared at all costs. Being prepared for the attacks is what keeps our hearts alive and well.

A wrestler at my son's school says it best. He is always looking forward no matter what is ahead of him. He hasn't lost a match in a few years. This kid is good, he's a really good wrestler and he's always prepared. I can imagine kids that have to wrestle him; they probably sweat over the schedule for months. The other day I saw this wrestler at the club; he's trying to make weight. I asked him, who he was to wrestle tonight? He said, "You know I am not sure; I just get on the bus." That is how prepared he is it doesn't even matter who his competition is, he's just prepared when he gets on the bus. Just like us, we know who our competition is, we just have to be prepared.

That's how we have to live our daily lives, being prepared to get on the bus. Being prepared to face the evil of this world every day, and this can come in many different forms. It can be through work, through family, through stress, and just plain fighting with our inner selves. That is where the stress comes from sometimes, just trying to figure out how we can make it through each day. That is where we need to be prepared, where reading the Bible and daily devotions really come in strong. You need to come up with the daily game plan to fight off evil as you trust Jesus and believe His word.

Remember Jesus plus nothing equals everything. I think we need to realize, that being prepared to face temptation is everything. There's more at stake than what we think what temptation can cost us. Our confidence in God, overcomes our daily temptations. We need to really decipher what the differences between a mistake that we make and a sin that we commit. Especially the sins we know we have committed. We need to cooperate with God and try not to manipulate God.

Remember He gave us the earth, and we have to invite Him into our house, He just doesn't show up every day without an invitation. Got what God wants us to meet us in each every area, like the bucket you be reading about later on this chapter's that is where He wants to meet us where we are struggling. But we need to invite Him into each one of these areas. We cannot do it alone. And when you're faithful in what God wants you to do, and then He will visit you in that place. I remember God delights in mercy, He wants to forgive us He died for our sins, but He also doesn't want us to purposely sin. And this is all part of Heavens faith in the Holy Spirit being gracious to one another.

Sin is one of the hardest things to combat in our daily lives we are constantly being bombarded with temptations. And when these temptations come upon us, we have to stop and think. If I make these decisions to turn toward sin, how my sins would destroy my family. That is where we need to really look in the mirror, is when the wolves are knocking on our door. We need to really realize what the consequences of our sins are, and stop our sin right there. Believe me this is not easy, I struggle with that each and every day. But I'm starting to recognize what my sins are, and I'm really trying to ask the Holy Spirit to intercede and walk away from sin. This is the point I think we all need to work on, it goes back to that being prepared and having that foundation we can stand on each and every day. If you're been on vacation been away from home, when you different setting and days past and you haven't even prayed. I have those moments many times; it is difficult and is hard to battle through those moments. I think the best way to make a wise decision is to ask myself if I am making a decision right now for me only, or is what I'm about to do going to be shared in eternity. I think that is the real question.

We need to be equipped for each and every day. We have the Bible for instruction to live a righteous life and spiritual growth. Just as a car has a manual, any product has an instruction book, and we have the Bible. It says in 2 Timothy 3:12 we need to continue to press forward from what we have learned. We all feel the trials and tribulations of everyday life, we've chosen to live with the instruction manual that God has given us. All scriptures are given by the inspiration of God. We continue to read the Bible, and be inspired by the word we will learn each and every day, knowing that we can face the trials with God on our side. I love this verse talking about sin: *2 Chronicles 7:14 "If my people, who are called by my name, will humble themselves and pray and seek my face and turn from their wicked ways, then I will hear from Heaven, and I will forgive their sin and will heal their land."* I think the key word is humble; we really need to eat some humble pie every day. There are a lot of people that just don't humble themselves before the Lord. We should do this every chance we get, and ask for His favor.

Another way I look at sin is to look at a wall. If you stand on the wall one side is a garbage pit, full of nasty garbage and things that have no meaning for your life. On the other side of the wall is a beautiful field, imagine the most beautiful field you can think of with green pastures and flowing waterfalls. So you're looking at the sin you're about to commit, you want to jump in the garbage pit or jump in the beautiful field full of wonderful things. It sounds simple to look at it this way but it isn't, like the wolf in the beginning of the chapter. If you jump into the pit it consumes you, and the more it consumes you, the harder it is to get out of the pit. Luke is one of our youth pastors at church, and one night he was speaking these thought-provoking words. The decision you're about to make, they will be talking about in eternity; nobody here will care about the decision you're about to make in eternity. I love that way of looking at things. Is this decision going to affect you for the rest your life in a positive way or in a negative way? Throughout the Bible, a plumb line is mentioned several times. I think this is Jesus way soon standing on the wall, or standing between two decisions of right or wrong.

We also need to look at each other, and build each other up in community in order to really keep ourselves occupied and staying away from some of the things that make us sin. I have a couple friends right now, and I'm really proud of the way they are living their lives. My friend Dave lost his job as a sales manager is working now for a big retail store at about a third of the income. I consider him being in community. He is satisfied with his position, smiling and sharing with others. I just talked to him the other day, he feels he is really meant to be there, working in the position he is now. I call this making tents, it's when God calls us to do something when we really know we really feel it's right. People like Dave are constantly inspiring me to be more trusting in God. Dave doesn't wear his faith 24/7 but he believes it each and everyday by the trust he has in God.

My friend Mark had a really good marketing position and was laid off, he looked for a job for almost 2 years and finally he decided to just do some woodworking and construction work with a friend. It is really keeping his mind occupied, he's not around others like Dave is, but is keeping himself busy and occupied. Thus keeping them away from being bored in keeping them away from the temptations of everyday sin that can enter his life. I think there are a lot of people like this; they're out of work, their home collecting unemployment and on food stamps, they feel sorry for themselves and they really can't find a way to make a change. That's when I see people like Mark and Dave that are making tents it really makes me feel better about how the world should be, and how we should strive to help one another. I look back to when I was a child, my father had three jobs and he was constantly doing whatever he could to support the family. Through those jobs I know he staying in community, being around others that help support him and his daily life.

Staying busy, I think we can focus on our community or having hobbies or things to occupy our time in a great way to keep our minds off of sin. I love you being occupied outside, and find that sweet spot regularly to be in tune with nature and God. That is where I first said the prayer that led me to even thinking about this book. I was in my backyard in that quiet place, working and doing things that kept me away from the places where I sin and am tempted. That's the main thing is avoidance if there's a room or a computer, pray that you won't go in there. Pray you will use the computer for the use it's meant for and not for things that will bring you down. The crazy thing temptation is everywhere; just watch Super Bowl ads, or ads anytime on television. These ads are crazy and all they do is promote sex, but that is the world we live in, and it's only getting worse. That's why I think it's so important to be in community, and have a support partner you can talk with about ever going online or doing things that are not in God's plan. An accountability partner is really important, and whenever you speaking out loud helps you realize what you are doing. They say if you tell somebody you want to lose weight, and you mention to somebody that you're going to lose weight, you have a lot better chance of losing weight. Anytime we can confess something out loud will only help us achieve our goals.

And the number one thing to do is to pray about it each and every day. When I wake up in the morning I always say the Lord's prayer. "Lead us not temptation but deliver us from evil thine is the kingdom," that is a great way to start out each and every day. If you have a chance to listen to Tony Campello, he talks about his mornings. The no time like Heaven theory, that God is eternal and everything happens simultaneously is something he believes in, and when he wakes up that's the first thing he does talks to God about his day. He even brings it so far, is to say that there is no time in Heaven everything happens simultaneously, that Jesus is on the cross that very minute and is forgiving me for all my sins. I know that's hard to grasp, but the way he explains it really makes some sense. I think it's so important to start out each day with a prayer and devotion. I go to our daily bread, www.odb.org and I am inspired by a quick story, and some Bible verses to follow it up. That's the most important things to build that foundation each and every day; otherwise the Wolf's will eat you alive. I have heard this from others before, and hours before we wake up the enemy is plotting ways to take us down. The enemy knows exactly where he can get us and how we can take us down. So their way ahead of you and your day, so I think it's best to get up and start the positive prayer that will help you throughout the day. There are many days when I'm sucked into the vapor sin, and it's hard not to get taken over by it. But the main thing is to be proactive and ask God for guidance and protection.

One of the areas when I really dig in deep, is dealing with the whole concept of Psalm 23. My friend Mark is really starting this right now, and understanding how simple but how deep it gets. It starts out the Lord is my shepherd, that simple word the Lord is my shepherd, and the shepherd that watches His flock. The shepherd stands over His flock and protects them. He is guarding them with His life, each and every day. The Good Shepherd is always watching over us each and every day. He guards us with His life; Jesus gave His own life to protect us and to be with us in Heaven. It's the same concept is the shepherd watching over sheep. When you can't do it yourself, and you feel both temptations ask the good Shepherd to protect you every day. Ask Him to protect you with His armor, the armor of God.

I think that's the best way, to understand how to be delivered from sin. Just ask for that protection each and every day. I think also when we are under the good Shepherd and we ask for His strength we can do anything. Each and every day prayer is so important; we need to be continually asking for protection and strength. Always looking for guidance through the complications in the chaos of this world we live in. I just take it a day at a time, not wondering through life waiting to stumble. But facing life and being prepared for battle.

CHAPTER 4 A Calling Spirit
What's My Line

1 Corinthians 6:11 - Some of you were once like that. But you were cleansed; you were made holy; you were made right with God by calling on the name of the Lord Jesus Christ and by the Spirit of our God.

Finding your true spiritual center isn't easy; you have to wait on the spirit. There have been several times that the Spirit has spoken to me, and it was when I least expected it.

Intercession on Feb. 12, 2011, I was not expecting anything from God that day. I was going to a prayer gathering to support my friend Mike. I remember when I first sat down, I was mainly thinking how important it was to be there for support, but also I was thinking of the time that I would be there and how long before I could get on with my day.

That is where I think we all fall way short, being honest with one another. There have been many times when I have been brushing my teeth and thinking about the many places the Holy Spirit shows up—Prayer Force, Career Connections, Madan in India, Praying with Tim's Group, Coaching at Hosanna, Trip to Honduras, Fundraising for Agua Viva and several times in just regular situations.

Asking God if I was nuts at McDonalds one day, then Him answering with one of the craziest spiritual moments I have ever had. Yes, one day at McDonald's are you kidding me. I was driving around town doing tons of things to get the fundraising started for Auga Viva and trying to do my regular sales stuff. I'll try a few things for work and on that Friday I was driving down Hwy 494 in Bloomington, MN. As Jim Cymbala says, this is exactly how this happened, if it didn't God strike me down right now!

I hadn't eaten lunch, and if you know me not eating until 2:00 PM, I was hungry. There is a McDonald's right off of 494 and Penn Ave. I sat in a booth with my coffee and quick sandwich. I sat in a booth facing Best Buy's corporate office. I sat in a booth facing the giant building. Best Buy was a huge opportunity for me in the sign business. I had been cold calling them for several months and had some success with emails and short conversations. This is where this just gets so down right crazy. I finished eating my sandwich and put both hands on the table and asked God if I was wasting time that entire week, was I actually going a little bit overboard. I just asked Him to show me a sign that this was all about Him, and it was real. I was doing everything for Auga Viva and trying to get all these things going.

I didn't want to let Jay from Auga Viva down; I wanted to attack this with everything I had. God was guiding me, and I was LETTING Him guide my every move. I bowed my head and said a 30 second prayer. I want to find out, right there and then if I was going crazy or if God wanted to work through me to help this trip. I bowed my head and prayed, "God show me a sign that this is all about You, not me, all about Your glory." I raised my head and was sitting in a booth staring right at Best Buy's corporate office. Yes, staring at the big yellow "Best Buy" logo. My phone was flashing.

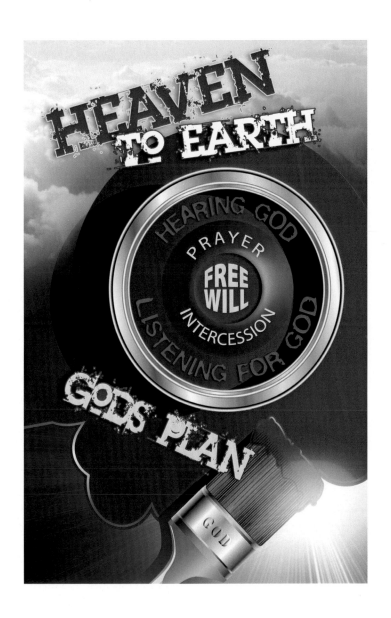

I answered it and hello this is Scott can I help you. I did notice it was a 612 area code because nothing came up on the area code. So I knew it was Minneapolis or Richfield. The voice on the other end said, this was Mark from Best Buy. Now if the call ended there it would be in the book that would be enough of a sign. Me asking for a sign from God, something to show me I am doing this for His glory, as I ask Him for one and Mark from Best Buy calls as I am Staring at the Best Buy logo. You know it didn't, it started as a small snowball and started growing and growing.

Mark said on the other end of the phone, "I saw an email trail from you and I recognized your name." He was interested in our products. I had been trying to get in as a vendor at Best Buy for over 2 years. Then he said, this is a strange call, I know you from the past. He told me his last name, and I tried to remember where he was from, and he said the last name again and I still didn't remember where I had met him. I said, did you go to my high school? Did we work together?

Then he gave me a third try, no luck. He said "This is weird, but I bought my house from you, the one in Burnsville." It was the only house I've ever sold. He said he wanted to get me into Best Buy. He said, "Can you meet with me next Friday?" At this point my head is ready to explode, I stayed as calm as possible. I didn't tell him what had just happened. It even gets crazier. He also explained how hard it was to be a vender at Best Buy and it could take a while to get everything set up.

I didn't care; I was just blown away by the last 5 minutes. I did meet with him the next week, and we had an awesome meeting. The snow ball gets bigger. When we talk about buckets in this book, my home bucket can be a disaster when it comes to my temper. I meditated on what had happened and I tried to pull out the true meaning and understanding of what God was trying to explain to me through this moment. That is what we all have to do—meditate on moments. Listen to God. God is trying to shape us and teach us all the time. Through experience, living, visions, and dreams. His greatness is everywhere; we all can make these connections. We all don't need a whirlpool story; we just need to be provoked. And start making our own circles and circle connecting to the light (ccl's).

I put the phone down and thanked God for the wonderful sign, a sign that only He could have created. I really started to think what God was trying to show me through that call, and that absolute miracle. Now as I have realized what that phone call meant to my faith and marriage, and what God was showing me. It just blows my mind away. When we met the next week, Mark from Best Buy explained to me how the info on all the products around the house has been great, especially the sticky notes all over the basement showing what electrical breakers and how the heating vents all worked. Mark bought up in the meeting that Friday how thankful he was that we did that, and I was to ask my wife how one of the vents worked. Some of the other people in the meeting thought that was funny.

As I meditated on this story and that night 8 years ago when we were moving from our first home, and why God was showing this to me. The closing of the house was the next day, we hadn't met Mark and his wife yet, and we were cleaning, packing, and getting the place ready. Very stressful, we have all been there. I went down stairs and saw my wife putting sticky notes all over the place, I yelled at her, like I do a lot. One of the things I pray for each and every day, for my temper to gets better. It has gotten better, but is still my biggest hurdle to get over in my family.

To live like Christ. Back to that night we were packing. When I saw her putting these sticky notes all over, my comment was, "What are you doing? We will never see these people ever again. Why would you sit down here and put notes all over the house when we will never see them again." I walked up to the garage pouting like a little five-year-old and told myself she's crazy. I remember standing there packing boxes just getting really upset and why would she take time to do this, and I never thought about that moment again until I started to write this book. We have a ton of packing to do; this is a total waste of time. I have looked at this moment in time an answer to prayer. It took about two months to figure out that God just didn't show me a miracle; He showed me one of my most defying sins.

I am not going to claim I am perfect with my temper, but I do know one thing I'm getting better. I truly believe that when I asked the Holy Spirit to show me a sign when I was sitting there that day, He did. This last summer my daughter was home from college, and I had one of my moments. Usually when I have one of my temper moments I stomp out of the house and go for a drive. This particular day I didn't, I stayed in the house and just sat there and thought about how angry I become. I still pouted, and said some nasty things to my wife. But I think the real breakthrough, was when my daughter Kippen came in the kitchen and said you're still here? I thought you left because I heard you yelling and mom. I told her that I'm trying to change, and God has put me on a path to change. I think that was the moment when I realized God doesn't change and He makes us closer to Him by getting over these hurdles.

I haven't done any business with the Best Buy Company since our meeting. Who cares, I didn't ask God for business, I asked Him for a sign that it was OK, I was just happy I wasn't going nuts. God showed me some other things, especially how I talk and treat my wife. She is an absolute precious gift from God. My life is so blessed by her strength each and every day. She keeps our family together and has always been there for me. Even when I yell at her or turn away from her, sounds like someone else I know, WOW. I just realized that as I am writing this how Christ like my wife is when it comes to our relationship. The sign and story brought the bucket idea to light; you will learn more how the buckets can transform your life. Mostly the balancing act we all face.

My story of how God has shown me the power of the Holy Spirit in my life on Feb. 12th. The journey is always happening and will never end, I mean never! I will share thoughts of what I think is important steps in this journey. I will also have others relate to me with their stories. That is a story in its self. How we have to start seeing God in others. Everyone has stories of how God is making their lives more complete and seeing Him through everything we do. God is everywhere and He is speaking to us all the time, we have to all start recognizing that, we need to restore this world, for all the future generations. This is not the responsibility of others, it is our responsibility. We can really do this, if an everyday person like me can start seeing the Spirit work each and every day, then you can also experience this living. It starts with small steps and believing with all your heart God's Spirit is living inside you. We need to start connecting our circles and make change through prayer and intercession. This is how restoration starts and it never ends.

I want to make sure you understand, I don't run around telling stories and claiming that I know anything more than anybody else. But I do understand that God has a plan for me. And I try to listen to the Holy Spirit whenever I can. But I really think that you can't ask the Spirit to come to you, you can't just turn on and off like a light like a light switch. If I sat here every day and asked the Holy Spirit to come in me and show me a sign, it wouldn't happen. But I do ask the Holy Spirit to come in to me and do miracles and speak to me just like He is right now. These are all times when I didn't know the Spirit was at work, but now I know. He is working all the time.

When I was writing this book from day one, I was always trying to figure out what its purpose was and why I was writing the pages. I had many days that I had thoughts that really I wasn't the right person to step into these stories. I don't know all the stories in the bible, I haven't memorized very many verses so why me?

One morning when I was up brushing my teeth I had this wave of emotion that was OK not to write this, but I knew I was supposed to and keep my eye on the faith that drove me out of that whirlpool on Feb 12th. I really had a feeling that if I don't write this it is OK, but I knew if I didn't I would not be glorifying God. I was struggling with this for days, and then I had a wonderful conversation with my friend Tim. Tim is in the middle of making a movie about the Exodus and he just wants to glorify God. He had been called by the Holy Spirit to make the movie that will bring many to the faith of Jesus, and tell the truth of the story of God. We talked about trying to figure out why He picked us, especially me. I had struggled with this over and over for months, why is this happening to me, and why does God want me to write these stories to inspire others to come to the cross. He is the way for others to restore this world, to make Heaven as it is on earth.

Then Tim said something that really made me think, it almost blew me off my chair. He said, "Who knows we might be the second or third choice to write this book, or make the movie." That really made me think, and I was just so overwhelmed by what he was saying. God chooses whoever He wants to, and sometimes it just happens to be one of us. It is about God's favor and choosing us, this is so crazy in my eyes. But when we choose Him, He will choose us, coming to the cross is the only way we can see this. God sometimes gives us a map that doesn't make sense. But, His path will be smooth and rough, it is true nothing can separate us from God. But, we can choose to say no. Romans 9 says, God chooses us. We make ourselves available and He chooses us.

God reveals His Glory to us, once we choose Him and make Him Lord of our Lives. That brings me to a place, sitting in Honduras at 4:30 AM writing thoughts about this book, and the events that got me to serve and to be closer to Christ. Hours earlier I was sitting with my team of 9 on this trip. I was with 9 other students and Hondurans all for the same purpose of serving God. It is a true path of how we each got to this place, a small village in the middle of a third world country. One purpose, spreading God's glory through a water system that will save them from disease and illness that contaminated water brings.

This is the Exchanged Life we are all living, exchanging our worldly ways with letting God lead us, listening to Him in everyday life. This life brings Heaven to earth, as I had seen numerous times on the trip. The Heaven on earth world that we can all be a part of if we just let God be the Lord of our lives, and live for loving others. These moments just continue to multiply so that we restore this messed up place called earth. We are only going to change it one way, from the bottom up, not from the top down. We have to come together with these circles that have the Spirit leading, these circles create community and these communities build cities that are restored.

One way to building communities and churches that are united on the principles of the word of God, Spirit, and Prayer. I have seen prayer change lives, by building your entire world around it. God answers prayer and He intercedes in our lives if we ask Him to do that. We have to look at the hope we have in prayer and always ask for God's Glory to be lifted in our prayer. The circles made sense even more when I was humbled by the fundraising I was doing for Agua Viva. There was so much momentum gathered when we first put together our coupon books. I was so excited to get out and go door to door to raise money for Jay and the students going to Honduras.

I told Jay we were going to raise so much money for the trip. He kept telling me that selling coupons was hard, and there will be tons of rejection. That was quickly humbled as I walked door to door getting rejected for the coupons I was selling for $20.00. It really hit me when I was standing at our local grocery store on a Wednesday afternoon. I had contacted 2 other stores in town, both said no. Then I went to the neighborhood store and talked to the manager. He told me to come in on Wednesday afternoon, double coupon day. I set up my table around 2:00 and stood there for 3 and a half hours. At first I was super excited, then as time went by I realized people were just strolling by, not even looking over at me. I started to get frustrated, then around 5:00 I needed to get some treats for my teen group at church that night. So I grabbed my stuff and jumped in line, all the registers were full. It was double coupon day, I stood there thinking what is wrong with these people. They all had shopping carts full to the brim, and I was just getting madder by the minute, but then I realized I have not always given. I started to look from the inside out, and more about the journey of what I had seen, not what others were going through. Everyone is at different points in their walk, and we just cannot judge that.

One of the most remarkable things I have seen on my journey to being closer to God each and every day is intercessory prayer. Intercessory prayer is real; it is as real as looking at the blue sky, or a fresh plate of food. It is so real I see stories of people healing and calling for a change of behavior. On Feb 12th I saw the power of the Holy Spirit. Now I know these things are real, thru stories at PTM, Church Groups, Prayer Force, and some of my friends. I see the power and believe it. I remember asking my daughter Kippen what she thought of people speaking in tongues and prayer groups that had unbelievable encounters with the Holy Spirit. It happened with Kippen a few times at church camps were people started breaking out it prayer and speaking in tongues. I have witnessed people speaking in tongues and I have had some really neat experiences. I have also had a few experiences where Holy Spirit showed me that some of it wasn't real. Then I have had other times where it was so real I was overwhelmed by it all. My suggestion is to read about it in the bible and be very careful of how you approach it. I just know one thing for sure, if you cannot speak in tongues, don't claim you can. I know that is not a desire of God. It has to be real and genuine, and it has to be glorifying God.

I have seen so many people be transformed by intercessory prayer. Madan a man in our PTM group has always wanted to travel back to India and speak to his native people about Jesus.

He prayed for years, and we prayed as a group for months to have his green card approved so he could travel back to India. In his land they are broken in to levels of status, they start from the best class and work down to the people that have been cast out, the Dalits. These people are treated like dogs, pushed out into the worst part of India. An area where there is no food or running water. His heart has always ached for these people and getting back there to help them. There are over 300 million Dalits in India today, almost the entire population of the United States. So intercessory prayer was really needed to get Madan's situation turned around. Madan has been in the US for many years, serving with Billy Graham and other mission groups. In 2009 he applied for his green card and he had been praying ever since. That is one thing about calling on the Spirit, and asking for prayers answered. It doesn't always come right away or in the way you want it to happen.

Towards the end of 2011 Madan had told us his mom, who lives in India out with the Dalits, was getting really sick. She had a stroke and was in desperate need of prayer. One side of her body was in tough shape from the stroke. By the end of August things got much worse, so we prayed a lot for both Madan's mom to heal and for Madan to get his green card to visit her. We prayed for Madan and his green card for weeks, he actually had an interview scheduled for him and his family to get their green cards. Then we prayed one day after PTM, 4 of us stayed and asked the Holy Spirit to intercede in the situation. One of the women in the group said she felt that Madan's mom would be blessed when she saw him and would be healed.

That afternoon my friend Chris called a lawyer friend of his and found out some critical information about a temporary visa. Then things really started to happen, within days Madan was cleared to go and visit his mom.

That is how we need to pray every day, nothing else works. There has to be something that we give back to God in every prayer. Just praise is enough half the time. We need to thank Him every day. As Madan says we are just here for a short while. We came from God and we are going back to Him.

I love the seen in the movie "Cocoon" when the aliens zip off their bodies like a suit. That is exactly what we are; we are all just souls that live in side of a sinning human body. We visit it for a short time then we return right back to our Father in Heaven.

We have to believe that we have His spirit in us, the same Spirit that was in us from our spiritual birth, the same Spirit that was with Jesus on the cross, the same Spirit that parted the Red Sea. The Spirit is really that powerful. You will hear several stories of restoration in my 16 month journey. Some of these stories brought me to tears. They are all stories of human souls taking God's call and doing something for restoration by using one, ten, a hundred, or a thousand other souls to move a neighborhood, community, or city to making a difference.

We have to know what is true with all our hearts. Or we cannot do anything through Him. Go make a difference in your neighborhood, in your community, in your city, in your state, in your country, or in your world. As earth as it is in Heaven, we have to restore. As Gabe Lyons says, use the gifts God have given each one of us and go now. Get up out of the whirlpool.

There have been hundreds of stories on my 2-year journey of understanding the Holy Spirit. Stories that have just taken my faith and belief out of this world, and closer to Heaven. I haven't really changed as far as who I am, but I do really feel the Spirit moving in several areas of my life. In this book, you will learn about buckets, and how we need to find how we can improve them. I really am looking for God in every story. Why not, He is all and He is in all. I am only going to tell a few of them. The first step is to understand the Holy Spirit and who this person is, yes I said person. The Holy Spirit is real. Put your hand in front of your face, do you see it, that is as real as the Holy Spirit. There are 3 parts to the Trinity.

There are thousands and thousands of books on Jesus and God. But there are few books on the Holy Spirit, yet it has the same equal part as the other 2 parts, God and Jesus. When you look at this, go get a glass of water and set in front of you. Now if can think of the 3 forms water (H_2O) comes in, liquid, Ice, and gas. Water is still water no matter which of these 3 forms. We can see the water and the ice, but the gas is all around us and we can't see it. I love this illustration because it is the best way to see a parallel line between the two ways to look at water and the Trinity. The Holy Spirit is inside all of us, it just needs to be jump started when you confess what it says in Romans 10:9, believe with your heart that Jesus is Lord. At the point of awaking the Holy Spirit, now it is learning how to tap into this eternal all powerful energy. I Knew it was there, but I had no idea of its power.

Before Jesus went to the cross, He said to the disciples, He was leaving this place on Earth and His Spirit will live on in everyone who believes in Him. This is where the rubber hits the road, think if He didn't do this. He also said you will be better off with me gone, and the disciples didn't like that He was going to be with the Father in Heaven. Can you imagine if this transition didn't happen. If Jesus would have stayed and not sent the Holy Spirit, He would be the most popular person on the face of the earth. Just think if you needed to be healed or if you needed Him in a crisis. What would you do? You would call His secretary and say, "Can I have Jesus for prayer sometime?" The answer would be He is booked up for the next 20 years, He has 10 minutes on June 4, 2035. Would that work for you Mr. Gulsvig, around 8:00. He will only have about 5 minutes and that is it, would 8:10 to 8:15 work for you? By the way there will be 10,000 other people in line, so please be patient. Think of the way we worship an athlete or a rock star, that would be how it would look. No, that is not what He did, He sent His Spirit and told the men you will be better off and we are because we can call on Him anytime any place. Wow, how cool is that!

That is the Spirit I am becoming better and better friends with each day as I grow. Yes, I said it. Better and better friends, that is how I look at it, my relationship with the Holy Spirit. Think of a close friend you have right now, did you become best friends after 15 minutes of coffee. No, it took a long time to get to know each other and all of the special things that allowed you to trust the other person. That is how this works, its all about trust and love for one another. I am at the point right now, I consider the Holy Spirit like a friend I can call and ask questions, or help me when I am down. Think of 10 people in your life you could call right now, if you where in a crisis. For me it is so simple, easy to think of 10 trusting people that never lie to me and always tell the truth. The friends that tell you things and always come through in a pinch. I can tell you I am not always that person. I have let many many people down in my lifetime, but I am trying to be better and live a life of truth and understanding.

That is how the Holy Spirit works in my life, I can turn and pray anytime, and any place. One thing I have learned is that we can't just ask when we are not present with Him. There needs to be a cleaning of our hearts before we approach the alter. Just toss that baggage out the window and trust that He will listen and answer in His time. I think that a lot of Christians that know who the Holy Spirit is, but they just have to have faith in the Holy Spirit. And we also have to have faith in what God is calling us to do, that is when the Holy Spirit will visit. My journey has been really awesome, we are all on this journey together. The connection to one another is the part that just blows my mind, the community of others and the power of the Holy Spirit is what makes this journey the most exciting. Now I would like to share not only my stories but others that have impacted me and my life through the Holy Spirit. You have to find ways to train yourself to hear God. I have joked with friend Madan, that he has one of those old fashioned homemade telephones, two cans attached by one string. One end he speaks into and the other God is listening. We need to learn how to pray like my friend Madan, forgive our hearts and empty our minds. I think it's really just about asking the Spirit to show us to listen to Him at all times with everything we do. And I think when you have this attitude and when you're looking at Scripture, He will speak.

Ask Him to show us the right things—NOT the things to just satisfy us, but the ones that make us better people.

CHAPTER 5

Coming Together
Connecting the Dots

2 Thessalonians 2:1 - Now we beseech you, brethren, by the coming of our Lord Jesus Christ, and by our gathering together unto Him

Connecting the dots, was the first thing I thought the story would be about. I had several people telling me that was connecting dots. When I first realized that something was moving inside me, I hadn't really realized that the Holy Spirit continued to move through me. I did realize that there were things restarting to connect. At first I thought it was just me connecting with new people then I realized it was more than that. One day I was sitting at work trying to complete some tasks and was thinking about all the people I've met since February 12, 2011. I was thinking of the two prayer group sizes that I now associated with, and how God was moving in several areas in my life.

I started to think about how these were all connected. Like I said I had several people that were saying God is just connecting the dots. But then I realized He was also connecting the dots, forming circles. Circles of friends and associates, and future connections. The circles can't work by themselves, we have to be connected together. Two of us connected with this connection also makes synergy which provides the power to change the world.

I look at some of the communities I am a part of right now. When you are doing things with the Holy Spirit, partners in prayer, neat things happen. Sometimes we see things that are being created for God's glory and purpose. His master plan, that will happen no matter if we are involved or not. I look at Agua Viva and those groups of men who listened to the plan God had for the people of Honduras, and how lives and entire villages are being changed. When we went there as a group last year, things happened that you couldn't explain. The power of the Holy Spirit was present in situations. It was a community of believers connected together for a common cause, to bring water to this community and to tell them about the Jesus that we knew and loved.

That seed was started with one person and connecting with 4 people in his small group. That group was touched by the Holy Spirit that lead to a team coming together to start the trips to Honduras. Now look at how the circles are spread out across the globe. The connections that it has created are mind boggling. I look at how people from villages in Honduras become part of teams that help new communities and help build water projects. Amazing is seeing this coming from a few circles connecting together and listening to that voice of the Holy Spirit that will lead us to great places. There can be one circle with one person speaking to 12,000 people, and there can be another circle with one person and one other person or there can be three people all of the circle or there can be four circles connecting together. The circles connect when the bond is formed.

I have seen this happen more than once in my life. I attended a church class called Financial Peace University.

This class teaches you about money, how to manage money and how to stay on track. Because what it does is it teaches you that if you manage your money you can manage your life and you'll have less stress therefore you can spend more time spiritually. Dave Ramsey the teacher of the class talked in length about how this will help you spiritually. At first when my wife said we were signing up I resisted, then she convinced me to attend. I am not taking any credit for how this story turns out, but I do see God had a plan through all of it, He knew the outcome before it was finished. He is still building on the plan, and it is awesome to watch it come together.

We attended the first 3 weeks and we really enjoyed getting together with our small group within the class for discussion. There was about 200 plus people attending the class at Hosanna Lutheran Church. We were the oldest couple in our group, but we really enjoyed listening to the stories of younger couples. It really made me think of our younger years. After the 3rd week my wife and I were walking out of the church and we ran into our good friend, Mark. He was attending the class also and explained how there were six people unemployed sitting at his table in class. The first thing I wondered was how they could attend the Financial Peace University class if they didn't have a job. 6 out of the 10 people at this table were not working. I thought of how sad that was for those people. That night on the ride home I talked to Keri about it, and I realized that has to be something that needed to be addressed. Then later that week I was provoked by God to come up with some type of a sheet that people could sign up for in the class and others could help them get jobs. I was driving down Highway 100 in the Twin Cities, just a normal afternoon. I started to think about those unemployed people in the class. I was just planning on making the connections, between the people in the room that had jobs and those people who didn't have jobs. Then I remember the number 5 in this feeling I had towards helping others in the class, was the Holy Spirit telling me there would be 5 jobs. No way this stuff doesn't happen to me, it was crazy the feeling I had to go home and start planning how to start helping.

The class came around, and I was sitting in class waiting for it to start. I came up with some forms that people could fill out with their name, the type of job they wanted, the position they were looking for, and include their e-mail. I had the sheets ready to go, but it just didn't feel right. I didn't tell my wife, I just planned on standing up during the sharing time in the beginning. But then as always I was starting to chicken out, I kept thinking "is this really from God?" As always in the class, the teacher would ask three questions about successes from the week before; if she asked the question no one seemed to respond.

She was standing there waiting for somebody to say something, then I stood up. Somebody came over to the microphone and I told the group what I wanted to do. Mark's table was clear across the room, so the first thing I did was share the information I had learned about unemployed people in the class. And I explained how they can practice Financial Peace University when they don't even have jobs. We need to see if we can help them, and if there were others, to please let us know. I passed around the forms, asking unemployed people to write down their name, phone number and e-mail. Then put the job you are looking for or the job you desire, and hopefully we could network and find you a job.

As I sat back down I wasn't very comfortable what I just said, my wife was just relieved I didn't say something dumb about our situation. Then the negatives started to rain in, I started telling myself that was a dumb thing to do. Like Keri always is, she was very supportive and said not to worry about it. At that point the second person stood and was talking about how they were selling things on eBay and they were putting the extra money away for future events. The entire time I was beating myself up about what I had just said to this big group. That person finished talking and I still felt I didn't really say what I wanted to say. I still felt stupid for standing up and saying something. Then it happened, a woman in the back of the room stood up. She grabbed the microphone and said she wanted to bless me and pray that doing this will bring jobs to the unemployed. That was the affirmation I was looking for, right there I knew God did tell me to do this and to follow it through. She also said that was really neat what that man was doing and all I did was in my mind give all the glory to God. When she said she wanted to pray for me, wow I was blown away. But the Holy Spirit was affirming that this was what I was supposed to do, and I felt so free from any guilt.

At this point I was blown away, I don't think I heard a minute of what the lesson was on that night, I was just excited to get the forms at the end of the night and start seeing how we could help these people. God had provoked me to take a step, to helping others. At the end of the night the forms were filled out and my wife and I went home to organize the data. My wife typed the information, and we were ready to hand them out the next week. We brought the forms back the following Thursday, after a minute announcement at the beginning of the class, we passed the unemployed list around the room. By the end of the 2 hour class people started talking about the jobs that were open, and connections they had in their community. Someone said a local phone company was hiring sales reps. Through this opportunity we started provoking the circle and it started to form and the people in the class started talking about a job sharing program. They all wanted to see what was happening and get involved. Over the next few weeks 3 jobs ended up being filled from the group.

Well during the time of this experience, I was involved in two prayer groups on Thursdays, one at 7 AM at Hosanna and one 11:30 with Prayer Transformation Ministries, at the same location where I experienced the intersession. At the 7 AM prayer group 2 weeks later, I shared this experience I had with the Holy Spirit. We started talking about how people must be unemployed and how we should pray for the unemployed. We are a big church, over 8,000 members, and we started to ask if unemployment is at 9.8% in Minnesota then there has to be close to 800 plus people that walk through our doors unemployed each week. As we talked a person in the prayer group Sharon, got very emotional. She shared that God had touched her in the same way and that the Holy Spirit was tugging on her heart too, she just didn't know where to start. She had been praying about it for months, so after the prayer time we met out in the lobby and talked about ways to get this a part of the church.

We met about it the following week and now initiating a group at Hosanna which is called the I-Team working for the unemployed. Now between Sharon and I we told the prayer group we were going to pursue this, Andy another person from the prayer group met with us. We just started praying and asking the Holy Spirit to help us form this group to help others. A group formed to help people get jobs those that are unemployed. These circles are continuous and the Holy Spirit connects the circles forming everywhere. Now the circles are touching one another and the circles of unemployment will start to be filled. Jobs will start to be filled. These are the circles with the synergy of the connection. Every month we have a meeting and pray for the unemployed, and try to make connections for people that are looking for jobs.

We later found out there had been a Career Connections Group that helped during our open house on Tuesday nights, we just decided to expand it to Saturday with more group discussion. It's absolutely amazing, seeing people getting jobs and transforming people's lives. One such story is Audrey, she came to our first Saturday meeting. This is connecting the dots and this is making the connections, coming together in the community to help one another. I think being in community with others is a great way to support one another not only in lifting each other up but studying God's word. For me personally I always think I'm getting around to studying or reading the word. I just don't find the time and every day chaotic life that I live. So when I meet with others, whether it be a prayer group, a Bible study group, or just fellowship, that's the time when I really feel connected. That is the coming together part. That is what's exciting, about being around others like this, just really pumps you up and makes you feel good about what we can do to make this world a better place.

It doesn't have to be named big either, just being together and discussing things that we already know. But then what happens is many other things trickle from those conversations. Even sometimes in a Sunday service, just being there and thinking through what the pastors are talking about really makes you realize that you can learn in any type of circle. In those connections it helps us become better Christians, and become better supporters of others and that helps us expand the circles by connecting with other circles.

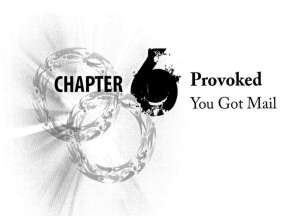

CHAPTER 6 **Provoked**
You Got Mail

Psalm 106:33 - *because they provoked his spirit, so that he spoke unadvisedly with his lips.*

Being proved and understanding when God is provoking you is so very important. It is also something you learn over time how to discern when He is asking you to follow Him. I don't claim to be an expert, not a chance. God doesn't talk to me like a voice that is speaking right to me, not a chance. But I can feel when He is asking me to do something for Him, and it is always affirmed by a verse or someone saying something to me. It is the provoking that got me started on this journey to write this book. Climbing out of that whirlpool has opened so many of God's doors that where probably there before, but I didn't recognize I needed to open them. All my life I just keep walking by one door after another. They were right in front of me each and every day, I was just too busy looking at other things of this world that distract us with each and every day.

Prayer Transformation Ministries (PTM) and Prayer Force have become a key part of my life each and every week. I have learned to listen to God through these ministries. I have also learned to step out in faith when I am being provoked with something small or big. Just like when I went on a mission trip to Honduras for 8 days. It just felt right to go at that time, since then I have been asked to go again, and the timing just isn't there. And that is OK, we can't force it, and get ahead of God. Being in some of these groups is a good opportunity to pray and listen to what God is telling me. I think we need to plug into spiritually connected groups like these. I have watched others and myself grow in these situations and learning times.

Both of these ministries have really become a true part of my walk to learn more about Christ, I just can't wait for Thursday's at this point in my life. Early every Thursday I spend an hour and a half at my church with the Prayer Force team at 7:00 Am in the morning, then attend a learning prayer time at noon with PTM. Everyone in both of these groups is sold out for learning more about learning how to pray, and praying through the Holy Spirit. About 7 months of spending each and every Thursday with PTM, I was sitting there praying with the group. One day a man named Tim came and shared information about a movie he was directing about the Exodus. It was extremely interesting and something sparked me about his talk. I went on the movies web site that evening. The site showed pictures of artifacts that linked to stories of the bible, Tim who is working on a film related to stories in the Bible. I was obsessed with finding out more about his project. I went on line and read some stuff about the movie, and watched some trailers that sparked my interest. One of the photos really tugged at my heart. So when Mark, one of the lead members of the PTM group, said Tim was going to share more about his project with our group, I was extremely excited.

Tim came to the PTM meeting and shared his vision of the movie. He presented his story. I was touched by his sincerity and the seriousness of the project. We all asked a few questions and he shared some pictures and maps from the points he was trying to convey in the film. I was really touched by the excitement of his voice in what he was trying to accomplish. He had been working on it for 10 years. He told awesome stories of how he was provoked to start the movie, and several stories that kept it going. I was really taken by his heart and how he felt led to make this movie. I was still trying to figure out how to decipher what is my conscience and what was the Holy Spirit. Even though I was provoked to get out of the whirlpool to attend my first intercession prayer, I still didn't know how to read the thoughts I was having, to direct me to listening.

Later that night I was home working on my computer and doing some things around the house. For some reason I stopped and then started listening to excerpts from Exodus and the verses he was trying to put with the film. Remember I don't read, I did use the online bible and the audio to go with it, and then I got to the plagues. Then I started to read and listen to more verses, some of the verses had to do with the Plagues against the Egyptians and Pharos wrath on the Israelite slaves. As I started to read the plaques I started to put together a list of them and how they related to the story. I couldn't believe I just put together this chart, for what reason? I emailed to Mark, Colleen, and Madan from PTM, and just asked them if any meaning came to them. Then what came of that to this day blows my mind. Mark ended up saying, "maybe we are supposed to go to Tim's office and pray." So we did the following Monday at noon.

We read the first chapter of Exodus and prayed for the movie. Since the noon prayer group has formed and we pray everyday to support Tim's staff in the making of the film. A few of us show up at noon at his office and pray for various things that the movie is working on. There is a core group of us and we each just show up when we can. That is being provoked. We have been praying daily for this movie for almost 3 years. We have read 12 books of the Bible, reading one chapter at a time. And we have things to pray for each and every day. The funniest part of all this, is Tim keeps thanking us for coming, and we keep telling him we get more out of this than he does. Which is 100% true, and on top of that I am realizing God is stretching my days to keep my work load in line.

Now let me take you to 4:30 AM, I am sitting in the middle of a wooded area writing in my journal in a small village in Honduras. Earlier that year in June, I had committed to this Trip to Honduras. I was provoked by God to be in that place at that very second. Not questioning why I was provoked, but trying to soak in what God had for me on the trip. Being provoked is what put me in the place I am writing this book, being provoked and following is what happens when you see the power of the Holy Spirit.

Being provoked can happen any place and anytime. I attended a funeral of a brother of my son's friend. Nicolas Payne was one of those great young adults that were taken to Heaven, way too early. Nick was a person that really understood what being provoked means. This was written in the memories in the bulletin at his service. He really touched me with this statement he made when he was 13 years old. When I read this, it really hit home of how we need to live our lives. He understood what being provoked was all about.

By Nick Payne:

Yes, the Bible does say that good works directly impact our reward in Heaven, but those works are assigned for us to do in advance, and nothing we do by ourselves will impact our reward. If an opportunity to do well comes up, then respond to it. God doesn't call us to sit on our behinds, but to look for chances to do well, and then to say "yes"! The Lord is our purpose and our identity. Every good deed that we do God actually has planned in advance for us to do. And when we follow through, our identity in Him will grow!

What beautiful words. I look at the mission of being provoked. Yes, mission! Every time we are provoked we are sent on a mission. That is what I am trying to share in this book, to be humble before God and just do a little more each and every day. That mission can be across the street to talk to a neighbor, or it can be us traveling around the world to build a school or new water well. The day I was pulled out of the whirlpool I was provoked by listening to God. Since then I have been training my heart to see what words or thoughts God is leading me to; are they just random ideas? But understand this, I am still not perfect. I don't listen when I should and I am still trying to make each day better, and trying to be nicer to others.

Recently I was at our PTM prayer group. I am just amazed by the way we can feel the leading of God to do something for restoration. I think of where I would be today if I would have stayed in the whirlpool that day. My life has taken a complete different path by being provoked. I have hundreds of new friends that I have met through radical thinking when it comes to faith and being provoked. I know the journey is the destination, and that is what is so exciting. Goals are important, but look at the journey as the destination.

Gabe Lyons, in his book "The Next Christians" he talks about being provoked. I was provoked one evening the week before Gabe Lyons was coming to our church. I was sitting at the computer Thursday before our Monday Lift Conference. I had heard our Pastors talk about the upcoming event and the speaker Gabe Lyons. I wasn't going to something like that? I was busy at work and they had it scheduled for a Monday. Anyway that Thursday night, I was looking for something on our church web site, and there popped up the Lift Conference logo, I clicked on it and read more about Gabe Lyons. I really liked his prospective on the Christian world today.

I signed up that night and told the guys at work on Friday I would be missing Monday, and I was missing some pretty important meetings. When I went to this conference and the minute Gabe Lyons started talking I knew we had a connection. I wanted to stop right there and sit down and ask him a bunch of questions. There have been 5 or 6 times in a public setting where I could just ask everyone else to leave the room, because it felt like the person was talking just to me! I remember one line that really stuck to me. He said, "I have been witnessing to my neighbor for 7 years and he doesn't even know it." He also explained how 18 to 34 year olds where just lost, even though the two faced Christians they knew personally had witnessed to them. That is where we all fall short, we need to show people we are Christians, NOT JUST TELL THEM!

I was sitting there just soaking it all in. He was on the same path I was on and it was really cool. That day, was one of those days when I sat there and realized the power of the Holy Spirit. Gabe is talking directly to me, I had about five or six of those moments I know from him last year and a half. Seriously, it is like nothing else in the room, no one else is in the room. It's very similar to what an athlete says he can hear the sound and can hear the crowd. I just sat there soaking it in, and I love the fact that Gabe never once said it was about him. It was all about glorifying God. When we glorify God the light spreads towards HIM I believe it's like a mirror that bounces right back on us. The more we do this, the more we get a touch of Heaven. It has to be about God it can't be about us. That's so hard for me to say, and so hard for me to live out in the flesh but I'm trying each and every day.

I still think back to that day on February 12, what if I didn't get out of the whirlpool, what if I didn't listen to the Spirit. With some of these things actually happened, would somebody also step up? I'll never know. Only God will know. But one thing I know, and I'm 100% sure of the people in my life that are now there have made my life so much richer. I look at dealing with the daily prayer at Tim's office, or being in prayer force or PTM each week, I can tell you I have seen these people, full of joy and the hope they have for making this world a better place. It's all about restoration, one person at a time, one soul at a time. This is time out of my day and life, but I always feel way more blessed.

One of the things I learned that morning getting out of the whirlpool is that there's a Spirit that is in us all the time. The Spirit is with us everywhere we go He helps lead us, He helps us make decisions. Being in the room at PTM, I thought and felt the Spirit move through me through prayer. At that exact moment I realize that God is the King and He does have a Spirit that lives in me. This is an easy way to understand it:

GOD (Father)- all creation of all things

JESUS (son) - God's only son, His only child. God sent Him on earth to die and free us from our sins.

HOLY SPIRIT (In All Things) - the Holy Spirit is our path between us and Jesus. It is our connection on earth that all of our prayers are sent to Jesus and our father.

"Our father who art in Heaven hallowed be thy name thy kingdom come thy will be done on earth as it is in Heaven." That is the key on earth, as in Heaven. "Give us today our daily bread." Lord gives us your word, some people make it so complicated but it's easy to get. Then He goes on to say, "Deliver us from evil, and lead us to not into temptation." It is as simple as living this and remembering it daily, please don't make it any more complicated than that. We need to remember Romans 10:9 when we are witnessing. Believe in your heart and confess with your lips that Jesus is Lord, and you will be saved. And remember the Lord's prayer each and every day. Remember those two things and the Holy Spirit will be working in you, ask the Holy Spirit each day to work in your life to grow God's kingdom. I recently heard Bono from U2 say the exact same thing. He loves the earth as it is in Heaven too! As God works His wonders through you by the Holy Spirit, please let others know your stories, and let your heart lead you to doing so. As God works His wonders through you by the Holy Spirirt, please send us your stories. Just go on www.10-9stories.org and register your story or upload your video. Those stories will be shared in future books and talks, people need to know God and what He is doing in the world, and of course give all the glory to God. I am still learning to share the stories I have lived, not to make myself any more important, but to share so others see hope in their daily lives.

When each group trains for trips to Honduras, we have meetings once a week for 10 to 12 weeks. In those 10 to 12 weeks, we talk and learn how God wants us to treat and help the poor. Many of us tell the stories that are experiences of how God works in our lives. My favorite part is when people share their testimonies. Some of the stories are so powerful. And you can't go on the trip until the entire group has heard your testimony. These testimonies are so powerful and believable. The way the Spirit works in people's lives it's everywhere, happening every second over and over and over all over the world. In every one of these people, they have an individual story, it really shows us how God created us as individuals. But also the stories, you'll find seed being planted, little stories of somebody going out of their way, listening to the Spirit. In Chapter 9 I will talk about planting seeds, this is what is planted from these stories. Sometimes a seed that is planted in someones life is just a small statement or gesture someone makes.

These testimonies help teach us the conflicts of others and they help us shape our stories and guide our lives, and provoke us to keep sharing and helping others.

God is constantly provoking us, we just have to learn to recognize it. I was talking a few nights ago with my friend Chris from church, he was telling me a story about a friend of his from high school. This is a friend he hasn't seen in almost 30 years. All of a sudden out of the blue he was provoked to share a book with him. His friend was going up to his hometown that next week. Chris looked up his friend, and had a nice visit and at the end said, "I was provoked to give you this book I just want to share with you." They both chatted for a while about the book, and then his friend said maybe it's smart to start a small group. We can have a study group centered on this book. Chris told me the last time he talked to him, they had started a small group sitting around a campfire once a week talking about the book. And I explained to my friend Chris how cool it is when you listen to the Spirit provoking you.

The same Holy Spirit, that lived with the 12 disciples and went straight to Heaven. He said to the disciples after spending 40 days with them after the resurrection. It is better I leave you now, and go to the father so I can leave my Spirit in each one of you. This is the Holy Spirit that provokes us, speaks to us, and gives me things to think about. There's only one Holy Spirit, the same Holy Spirit that spoke to Moses in the burning Bush. In the same Holy Spirit that parted the Red Sea, that's what so crazy about this, we have the ability to ask for the same Holy Spirit to help us. If we turn to the Holy Spirit and pray to the Holy Spirit that is when we can be touched by Him and taught by Him. It's like picking up the phone to call a friend. I call Rick a lot, whose did the illustrations for this book, I confide in him things about work and about things about the book. That is the same thing we can do with the Holy Spirit, pick up the phone, text Him, or send Him an email.

It really is that simple, asking for something, asking for help, and most of all asking for strength to help us through the battles we face each day. Because that's the main thing, we can't just say Holy Spirit give me all the answers on my test, even though I never studied. But we can ask, for strength where were starting, and that the words come to us easier. But we still have to use our hands and feet and put in the work, this is where a lot of people get really confused on how the Holy Spirit works. We still need to put the time in input the hard work in, and make sure at the same time we are asking the Holy Spirit to guide us. It says in the Bible that we will be working in Heaven, we are actually doing tasks and working together. So why wouldn't we be working on earth?

Asking the Holy Spirit for help, and prayer and asking for the invitation to become an intercessor in our lives is the most important step. He's just sitting there waiting for us to ask Him for His help. He is on call 24/7 and we don't use Him. A lot of times we just move ahead without a thought of the Holy Spirit. Especially in those buckets. I'm struggling the most at home, and being intentional at work and around friends. The growing process we just have to keep asking for His help, because He will give it to us and will come to our aid. But we still need to work hard at it, we still need to use our hands and feet. I praise God for all the times He's got me through the tough times in my life, and I praise Him for those times in the future when He will get me through those tough times again.

Also I explained to Him about other chapters, that when these things happen the connections do seem everlasting. I said what if someone in the group read that book, and is inspired by it and does the same thing I did. Handed to a friend I've known forever, see the diagram below of what could happen.

That's what's so cool about sharing this knowledge and sharing the Spirit. We'll never know what happens to that seed, that one seed could be a field of seeds. Just like when you order an apple orchard, and see rows and rows and rows of apple trees. We will never know when we will trust God what will happen. It's like going back to what Nick Payne said, the works we do are assigned to us in advance. God knows we are willing to do it. It's kind of like when I first decided to write this book, I knew I was supposed to do it. Even though I've never written a book, much less read a book, or even hardly write a paragraph.

I just knew I was being provoked, I knew I was to step out in faith write this for some reason I do know that it's baby steps each day closer to understanding what God has chosen for my life. That is one of the true meetings and true purposes I think of this book. I really hope that it convinces others who were just sitting in their seat at church weekly or biweekly basis. Hearing a great message but not knowing what to do with their gifts. It's like a flour sifter, just take all the gifts you think you have in your system and come up with two or three you know you're really good at, those gifts that you just love to do.

Some people are good at swinging a golf club, others are good at helping others, some are good at cooking, and have the gift of organization. Get creative, and pray how God wants you to use these gifts. I know there are hundreds and hundreds of men at our church that are very good at construction, I know they can swing a hammer and pound a nail with the best of them. I would love to just stand up in front at our church someday and just ask people to break into groups. Start by taking these groups and breaking them down. Who is good at what? The eight thousand members of our church all have a special gift from the Holy Spirit. It is up to people to show their gifts and how we as a church body can use each of them to grow the kingdom.

People have no clue, of how easy it is to step out, they're so busy with their day-to-day activities they think they don't have time. I'm thankful when I look at our Career Connections group at how many people it has touched. It is just crazy to think, that each of us have a gift. One person has a gift of organization, another one is really good at connecting people, to others who could be used as recruiters. When you break this down, it's just incredible how it all works. When these just come together to form a smaller group, it is amazing what happens. Take your gift, and use it for what it's for; helping God's ultimate plan. I say that, it just means to glorify God through your gift. Everyone has a gift, God created everyone on this earth, with a special gift. You just have to figure out what it is, and use it for His ultimate plan.

A lot of times when you're trying to figure out your gifts, ask someone else. Ask a friend or acquaintance what they think you're good at, and what you can bring to the table to help others. I can go right on the list of every friend I have and I can tell you without a shadow of a doubt what their gift is. I think of my friend Rick who's doing illustrations for this book, I realized God gave him an awesome gift of creativity. He is using this creativity on the illustrations he's also helped many people with their ideas and their missions.

Take for example of two women that he met through friends and acquaintances, I have this idea to do a Jesus doll. June and Amy got together and knew they loved kids and had passion for those that were scared at night. Kids that were scared of things hiding in the closet's, you know those things that most little kids are scared of, and they realize they needed something to hold onto. Well through many trials and tribulations they came up with a Jesus doll. It's a cute cuddly Jesus doll, and if you buy one, they donate one to a third world country. They recently just went to India and handed out hundreds of Jesus dolls. Now think of their spiritual gifts, their gift of reading to their kids, and calling their kids for bedtime. Would you realize that was a gift? Through prayer, stepping out, and being provoked; that's what June and Amy did.

So now there is this website www.goodnightshepherd. com we can go on, buy a doll, that not only is a great gift, but it also comes with the tag saying that you are donating one of these dolls along with that story to a child in a third world country. Now we go from being provoked, to being like the ripples we talked about another chapter. Can you imagine the ripples that are going out in every direction as one of these kids gets a doll? Not only does it help share the story of Jesus, but also of the child in a third world country to go to sleep, in peace at night. Talk about taking a gift, being provoked and fully doing God's plan.

There are thousands of stories I could write in this book, when I think about Agua Viva and when the group of four men in their Wednesday morning Bible study eight or nine years ago were sitting around thinking about how they could change the world. They each had unique gifts, but they did not know how to use them. So they prayed about it. In one of the groups, Frank kept hearing something about water. Frank was being provoked, just like we are all being provoked to use our gifts. So Frank stepped up at a Wednesday morning meeting and said, "We need to do something about water, and bringing water to others." So they started studying the teachings of living water, and the next thing you know, there are several water projects that have been completed in Honduras. They started a website called www.aguavivaonline.org and are continually helping to improve the water in villages, and also starting foster programs and scholarships for kids going to college in Honduras. They are also listening to the Holy Spirit on a possible health clinic.

I am very thankful that the Holy Spirit moved me out of the whirl pool, and into a life of believing the Holy Spirit can move in each one of us. It has helped me to keep me moving towards a better understanding of how God works. I would not be writing this book if I did not obey the prompting of God in my life. I look forward to the other challenges I will face in the future. I just pray I recognize when He asks me, I know I have missed many chances when I have had scales on my eyes. When I look at others like Jay, Frank, Dave, and

Loren from Auga Viva and the opportunity they have had to listen to the Holy Spirit. It just fires me up knowing we are all making a difference in a small way, but in a big way being a part of the body of Christ. Doing it all for God's glory, not for ours. It is just awesome what God can do with just a few people that just listen.

It's crazy to think of these ripples through being provoked just expand out in every direction, it's just awesome to think what God can do with just a few people being provoked. That is why, in this book one of my missions is to think of creative ways to provoke people to step out, not giant huge steps, but little baby steps that are easy to take. If you ever seen a baby crawl for the first time, that is what I am like right now. I am still in the growing stages. I'm letting God provoke me in many different areas. I am no way perfect, not even close. I need to fix many of my buckets, but it is a journey.

That's what's so exciting about all this. Watching others being provoked doing good things for the kingdom. Just think, years from now, hundreds of years from now we will be sitting around telling each other stories of how God provoked us and how we on earth accepted the challenge. Not changing the world with one giant mega swoop, but with one baby step, and one baby step at a time. When you add all these together, you get that giant wheel, that giant way God wants us to change the world. It can be changed through doing it together, through love and not through judging others.

I've mentioned this many times in the book, when Jesus left this earth, the last thing He said is to love one another and to use the power of the Holy Spirit. That is what's so cool about all this, when we take these baby steps and asked the Holy Spirit to help us, we can do things and He will help us. He wants us to do with hard work and with our hands and feet. He doesn't want us to just sit and wait for something to come. But He wants us to listen to His prompting from learning though His word and others to use our hands and feet. Just like when Frank from Agua Viva, telling the guys we need to do something with water, he was being provoked. He was going outside the boundaries, going outside the gate.

That is where it's hard sometimes. It's hard to go around and knock on doors on a cold Saturday afternoon selling coupons for mission trip. Those days I got the door slammed in my face more than once, but it was so rewarding somebody said yes, it made up for all the no's. We will face several hills and valleys when we follow the provoking of the Holy Spirit. But that is all part of the learning process, and becoming more like the person God wants us to be.

I think of helping others not only by physically helping them, but also praying for them and interceding in prayer for them when a need arises. This is when it all comes together. Heaven as it is on earth is exactly these moments. When we are in community we support one another with using our hands and feet and gifts to support them, but also to help them come alive in hope and protection through prayer and real support. Praying for them is one of the key aspects of the circles we live and grow up in. I get a real kick of energy when someone tells me they are praying for me. Almost like, now I can't lose. It really makes me feel good and it helps me to pray for them. I have a few friends that are continually sending me verses and things that build me up each day. Some of my friends almost know exactly the time when I need a shot in the arm, that is them being provoked to help others. It's just that simple.

I am not telling you that I spend hours and hours helping others. I have just increased my time spent helping others, and trying to do the right thing. I believe that is that main purpose of this book, is to show that a knuckle head like me can just step up and learn more about God and this journey we are on. I am trying to get better, one day at a time. Sure I am still trying to be a better husband and father. But also trying to just keep helping others and helping just a little to restore this world we live in.

CHAPTER 7 Praying Heart
Do it for His Glory

2 Chronicles 7:1 - *Now when Solomon had made an end of praying, the fire came down from Heaven, and consumed the burnt offering and the sacrifices; and the glory of the LORD filled the house.*

One of the hardest things I have seen on my journey to knowing God, is trying to keep my eyes on Jesus. It is a learning process to keep your eyes focused on Him. I usually take 3 steps forward and 2 back. I'm not trying to do it, it just happens during the chaos of everyday just gets in the way of my focus on Him. That is why it is so important to live in community and to learn from the Word. I think it is taking baby steps. Just saying you are going to read your Bible or pray more is not enough. You need to commit to others in community to force you to be in learning and prayer-filled situations.

Praying is not trying to wish things into existence, we still need hard work and dedication He wants us to do the work . He wants us to be involved. He wants us to learn from being involved, that is when the real growing happens. It happens with prayer, with others in community, or with others that are around us. Yes, there are times when we pray for things out of our control, but other times our prayers must be combined with work. I always try to pray that my actions will be part of His plan, that they will make this world a better place.

Like I said earlier, when we are provoked through the Holy Spirit we still need to use our hands and feet and get the work accomplished. We can't just sit there and hope or wish that it's just going to happen. We need to take action on what God is telling us, we take action and look to Jesus for His guidance. That is what prayer intercession is all about, is being able to turn to Jesus and ask Him to help change the outcome of a certain situation. I've seen prayer change people's lives and change the outcome of many situations. Especially when it comes to healing, I have seen people healed several times. Most of the time I pray that people just feel hope in their situation to pull them through the tough times. I strongly suggest, that you look to learning more about intercessory prayer. I am not even close to an expert on it, and I need to learn more. Recently one of the churches in our area had a multiple week course on intercessory prayer, but I was unable to attend. I plan on attending one sometime in the future and learn more on how intercessory prayer works.

I think it's like anything else, you need to study it and learn more about it. It's like any skill, why wouldn't you think you'd want to learn from others to get better at it. That's what's so funny about things that have to do with God in learning. It's just like anything it's a skill that we need to learn, but people think because it's religious to a different category we can't just go and learn. We learn to drive a car, we learn to play the piano, and we learn how to be a better golfer. Why can't we take a course on how to learn to be better at talking to God! In many of these teachings it's just stories of people, who experienced the fullness of intercessory prayer. That's it's cool about hearing of the stories, you know it works and you know that other people believe in it. Just like learning anything else it gives you confidence.

It is all really exciting to know that you can learn more about something, and be closer to knowing how God answers our prayers. Turn your eyes towards Jesus, just like the song. That is all He asks, to be learning more about Him each and every day, and turning our eyes towards Him in a number of different ways. When we stop and go back to salvation, sanctification, and service. The first step of salvation is really the baby step that puts us close to Jesus. At that point that is the closest point we are to Jesus, and throughout our lives we just take baby steps closer and closer to Him. I have a long long long journey ahead of me trying to be closer to Him. And I do realize I'm not perfect, I realize I have many faults. But if I'm trying to be closer to Him every day, that is all He asks and He can never be closer to us. He is always pursuing us. He can't love us any more than He already does. If you haven't studied the book of Romans, please read through those chapters, and try to figure out what I'm talking about!

When I first heard this, it was so hard for me to comprehend that Jesus can't love me anymore than He does right now, that's crazy talk. How is that possible, He loves me the same as anyone else on the face of this earth. Again you need to learn more, about Romans, and about what it says about how much He loves us. And that's the other part of the equation; we can't do any more, or be any more of a person once we turn our eyes towards Jesus. That's it, it's completed the work is done, once we turn our eyes towards Jesus we are in His kingdom. Heaven as it is on earth kingdom, and eternal life kingdom. When we turn our eyes to Jesus for the first time, that is salvation, and that is where everlasting life starts. Think how huge that is, we will never die, we will only die in the flesh but our souls will live forever and ever. Try to stop and think about how long for ever and ever is, it'll make your mind explode thinking about it.

We should pray with all our hearts, asking Jesus to work through us—the same Jesus who frees us from sin to live eternally with Him. He is asking us to take a step closer to Him each and every day. Baby steps, you have to think of it as baby steps. I love something that Tom Lehman the professional golfer once said, "I take two steps forward, to becoming a better golfer, but then I take three steps back." That is exactly what we do each and every day we want to be better people, we want to be closer to God, but we fall each and every day. And that is where prayer is the most important part, getting up each morning praying to God that we will love Him as our intercessor in our lives; and ask Him to help us in each area. Ask Him to help us get better at the buckets, so more buckets will be overflowing, and some will be almost empty. Praise Him for the ones that are overflowing, and ask for help in filling the others. Glory to His name!

Being around others that believe in intercessory prayer is enough for me, most of the time. I still get distracted by everyday things that get me off track. Remember, intercessory prayer is something we have all done since we were young. Praying for a safe night's sleep, that is intercessory prayer. As Charles Spurgeon says in his sermon on Intercessory Prayer all of the people in the bible prayed non-stop for God to Intercession in the lives and situations of others. In his Sermon he gave on August 12th, 1860 – True Prayer, True Power. It is the Spirit of Intercessory Prayer. Intercessory prayer is real; it is as real as looking at the sky or talking with a friend. Put your hand out in front of your face; look at it and you know it is real. Just as your hand is real in front of you, so is the Holy Spirit inside of you. Please believe this, this is the most important part of the connection to restoration is what he said, but most of us fall way short of believing we have this power inside us. We all have to believe, the minute we say we believe in God and all the power He has, we now have the Holy Spirit inside of us.

This past Easter I was flipping around the channels on Saturday night, this was a month or so after the Holy Spirit spoke through me at our prayer gathering. I came across the timeless movie The 10 Commandments. Moses was standing there in front of the burning bush, when God was instructing him for the good of His people. He was filled with a glow; I had a crazy thought at that time. That is the same Spirit that can talk through me; it is the same Spirit that lives in side of all of us as believers. We just have to wake it up, and understand how powerful it really can be. Since then I see the Lord's Spirit like that seen with Moses, it is in me all the time. The Spirit is my guide in writing this book.

This is a great story of my friend Madan; he was the person guiding the Spirit filled moment I had on Feb. 12th. He has taught me so much, and how to tap into our one and only Spirit. The Spirit that is inside each and every one of us; inside each of us for us to understand and help with the restoration of this place we call Earth. A true friend, Madan is constantly praying for my life and family. He has been in the country for years, and he is a true believer that life revolves around intercessory prayer and God's plan for each of our lives. Prayer Transformation Ministries (PTM) and Prayer Force stories have been an awesome part of my life, being in community that is full of Spirit filled people that trust that they live with the Spirit in their heart and soul.

You cannot deny these stories in this journey we are all on. They are true witnesses to what God is all about, and the Spirit is calling me through these events to put this all on paper. Madan's life story starts as a young teenager in India when he first woke up to the Holy Spirit. He grew up living in India with the Dalits; they are a group of people treated like dogs are pushed farther and farther away from society in a world where no one cares. The number in the millions, 99% of the time there is no way out.

Madan did get out, and he came to America through a National Mission group. He has hundreds of stories of how the Holy Spirit has been leading him on a journey to get him back to bring the gospel back to his people in India. When Madan first came to the country he was serving God working with the Staff of Billy Graham. He had the honor of learning how this great man has awakened millions of souls. When he left the Billy Graham foundation, he served missions in the Twin Cities metro area. Soon after that, Prayer transformation ministries were formed to help Christians form a bond in community and praying to intercede in people's lives. The stories and events that have transpired though this calling are truly miracles in many just normal everyday people's lives.

Madan wanted to go back to India to see his family at some point, so in the summer of 2009 the group from PTM started praying for Madan to receive his green card and have a chance to go back to India. They continued to pray month after month. In 2011 towards the end of the summer, Madan was told that his mom had suffered a stroke. Her left side was extremely weak and she was really not doing well. During one of our Tuesday prayer meetings 4 of us where praying and we prayed with focus on Madan and getting his green card and his chance to see his mom again. When we were praying, you could feel the Holy Spirit fill the room. One of the women said he would be traveling very soon. When we were finished and I was walking up the stairs, I felt a sense of the Spirit telling me it was going to be OK, and he was going to get to go to India.

Later in the week, a big break opened up for getting him to India. Madan and his family had been interviewed and fingerprinted so the green card was close. But, with his situation, he just couldn't wait any longer. During a time of Thursday prayer a friend of mine Chris, who now attended PTM started to think of ways to get this done. Ron another member of the group mentioned that you could get a temporary travel visa if you are already approved. Chris ran with this later in the day, calling a good lawyer friend that he had known for a while. Well after many calls and emails, Madan had the proper forms in his hands. At that point I just knew he was going, prayers would be answered.

The following Tuesday, I was driving to pick up a project from a client. Usually, I text Madan a few times a week for prayer requests and little messages to keep us thinking of the Spirit and how God is working in our lives. I had not had contact with him for a week. I hadn't sent him any notes because I knew he was busy trying to get his travel papers completed. Even though I didn't know either way, I had a sense that God was going to take care of him and his family. I was driving up north, and praying that he was organized and ready to go on this trip to India. When I was praying and could feel that God had touched my heart that he was going to be okay, and everything was going to work out. I stopped at a light and I had a sense to pull over and send a text to Madan. Remember I hadn't seen or heard from Madan in days. It was such a calming moment, so I did. Here is the exact text that went out and came back on that September afternoon.

9/26/11 2:29 PM To Madan: How are you?

9/26/11 2:31 PM From Madan: Yes, I am in the plane leaving in just a few minutes.

9/26/11 2:33 PM to Madan: WOW

9/26/11 2:36 PM from Madan: Yes, Bye Now!

That was the first moment I truly knew he was going to India. There were some of us praying for him and several of us in intercessory that this would all come together. This was the exact moment he actually left. There are many people that would say these chains of events are just a coincidence. That is fine, they can say that, but I know different. This was a perfect example of the Holy Spirit working through community and the love we need to be pouring on each other for God's Glory. How do you explain the fact that all these things just happened? When I look back at the community spirit-filled stories, I see God just pouring Himself out on these situations. I arrived at my vendor in the north side of the Twin Cities. I stood outside for a few minutes and thanked God for the glory He poured out to Madan and his family. I stood there, and there was a huge tree about 100 yards away just blowing in the wind.

I watched it and thought back to a scene from the movie - Phenomenon with John Travolta. He realizes that everything is connected, and the Spirit is all around us, it is everywhere. We watch in the trees in a scene, he says that were all connected and were all here for a reason. Everything is connected, if God created the Heavens and the earth, and created everything on earth. Then it is all connected back to Him. There is a purpose for all of it, and a purpose for us. The net praying heart; and praying for things as if they were all connected back to us. But it's all connected to God's greater plan. He has an ultimate plan for us. Part of that plan, is to make Heaven on earth.

Then I heard a plane in the distance, I saw a plane going in and out of the clouds. I was positive that was Madan off on his trip. He had just shut off his cell phone moments before, so I prayed for him and his trip to see his Mom. I felt a sense of calm come over me, and I realized the connections that put this in place. As I was standing in a parking lot, watching the plane that was destined for a place that happens every day at the exact same time, only this time my friend Madan was heading home. Only this time God's Spirit was in this flight, with a purpose for God's Glory. Then I had one of those whirlpool moments, what if I had never got out of that water, where would God's grace be in my life. How many hundreds of moments to see His glory would I be missing. That is how important it is to take that first step. The story of Madan's trip to visit his mom doesn't stop there, it just gets better. During the time he was there he prayed over his mom, and she got much better over his two week stay.

He also spoke in a local church; spoke the gospel in his native language. 100's of people came the first night, and then the following day more came to hear the news of Jesus. They all loved the fact that he was raised like one of them, and he was back to help them out of the darkness. Many people said "yes" to God during those many times he spoke to them. He ended up talking to over 3,000 people. Praise God! As I am writing this, he is planning on going back with his family in a month and is planning 3 big services where over 25,000 people will attend. Madan, through the grace of God, is going back to pull them out of the darkness. He also has plans to go back next year and talk to 1000's. This was God's plan from the beginning; he knew this was the way to get the word of Jesus into these remote areas. Like I always tell people, be careful what you ask for, if you are truly Glorifying God.

We are going to form a Prayer Team to pray for him when he is in India. He will truly bless the people, and give them hope. I was glad I had been to Honduras in this time since he went to India. My trip really helped me relate to what he sees over there. I know God wanted me to be able to see what I saw, so when I pray for Madan, I can truly relate to what he is seeing. Also, the type of person he is sharing the gospel with, poor people who want to listen. They just want to be loved. Who knows I might end up sleeping on a floor in India sometime soon. I will pray if God has a plan for me and others to spread the gospel to His true family.

Madan has been to India dozens of times, and when he goes he shares the gospel to hundreds of people. Some of his, teachings there have been in front of 5000 people in attendance, in an area where there is no hope. In an area of the Dalits, where no one wants to help these people, they're basically abandoned. That is where Madan was originally from. When he returns they find great comfort in seeing one of their own. He's going out to these people and sharing that there is hope, and people do care about them. Jesus cares most about them, and loves each one of them. Many people hear his stories and turn their eyes to Jesus during these teachings. Now he is working on radio spots that would broadcast all over parts of India, and finding ways to get Bibles to some of the smaller areas. Not just Bibles but Bibles on tape, and solar powered tape recorders to deliver messages.

What I find most amazing thing that this all started out of a group of 15 to 20 people, praying for him in a town in

Minnesota that could have been anywhere. Prayer works, it really does. I see it over and over. It could be just small prayer to heal a cold, or if huge prayer to send a man over to India to help save hundreds and thousands of souls. That's what's so amazing, all the prayers are part of God's ultimate plan, and that is why we have to give Him the glory. I'm not taking any of the glory writing this book. Did you read the beginning? I don't write, I don't read, and I surely don't have the patience to sit here writing right now. So I'm giving God the glory, for whatever this book accomplishes. If only one person reads it and changes the way they pray, and the way they are connected to others through the Holy Spirit, that will be enough for God's plan. That's all He asked, is for us to be connected and turning towards Him all the time.

One of the stories I shared with the people of Honduras, and a story I plan on sharing with the people of India if I ever have the privilege of going there with Madan. It is a great story of how the father loves us with just an easy question. Tell Him you love Him and He will love you back forever. I have been in the same bible study group for years. Ben from my group wrote the forward for this book. Many times we have challenged each other, to challenge each of us and our families. Once we had to pick a person in our family we grew up with, and pray they would start going to church. I needed to be praying for my brother Greg, and he ended up joining a church in his community.

The same Mike that I got out of the whirlpool to pray for on the 12th of February challenged us to hug our fathers the next time we saw them. The challenge was to hug and tell our fathers that we loved them. He had recently lost his father, and he was reflecting on what that meant to him. Well this wasn't so easy for me, my family really wasn't the hugging type,

I was nervous about doing this in front of family. My father lost his mom when he was 7 years old, and he was shipped out to relatives at a young age. I just assumed this would be hard for him also, but Mike kept reminding us, and I kept thinking about a game plan. When you think about it, how stupid it is to even think you can't tell a parent you love them. I had a game plan to hug my father. I think it was Thanksgiving, we had finished up the day, and we were getting ready to leave. I thought this is it, I can do this or Mike and the guys will ask me forever. I went over and hugged my Mom and then I walked over to my Dad and hugged him and I told him I loved him. To this day there is rarely a day when I see him I don't hug him and tell him I love him. It has been so cool over the years. I recently attended a volleyball game with him, and in the middle of the stands in front of a ton of people I hugged him and he said, "Love ya guy." I cannot tell you how great that makes me feel. It hard and stressful to take that first step and tell my Dad I loved him, but it was so easy. The love I have received in return will never leave my heart.

That is how hard and how easy it is to ask our Father in Heaven to love us; we just have to ask him once. From that point on He will love us, and tell us He loves us forever. That Holy Spirit will tell us through stories and miracles each and every day. This is my story of both my father's loving me back. They both loved me before I hugged them and told them. I loved them, they just return it back each time I hug them. I just can't believe how much more we receive back than we give. It is immeasurable; we will never know the value of asking our father once to ask him to hug us and to tell us He loves us.

The circles made sense even more when I was humbled by the fundraising I was doing for Agua Viva. There was so much momentum gathered when I first put together our coupon book. I was so excited to get out and go door to door to raise money for Jay and the students going to Honduras. That was quickly humbled as I walked door to door getting rejected for the coupons I was selling for $20.00. It really hit me when I standing at our local grocery store on a Wednesday afternoon. I had contacted 2 other stores in town, both said no. Then I went to Rainbow foods and talked to the manager. He said come in Wednesday. It didn't go well in my eyes, I only sold 2 coupons in 3 hours. I was standing there all by myself praying about how God was good, showing me that day to humble myself and be happy with what has been given to me. I will never forget what happened the rest of that day. God did show me how to humble myself, and how to give Him the glory or what I was doing.

The funny thing is, that is a day I will never forget. I will never forget standing there watching these people walked by me one after another and not buying the coupon. When I did finally start walking in the store I stood there looking at all the people in line. It was double coupon day, and the place is packed. I asked myself why these people were not buying my coupon as they walked about spending hundreds of dollars. Then God hit me with something; I give every time I have a chance, but how many times have I walked by somebody trying to raise money for a cause. It struck me, like a hammer hitting me over the head. It made me really realize, people are busy, and people are not always looking to help others. I am not always looking to help others. I prayed for a lesson and I received a lesson I will never forget that day.

A couple of days later I pulled up to my normal place for coffee just miles from my house. A man said to a stranger, "you live a great life everyday" The stranger said, "I am trying to wish it into existence." Wishes into existence, that is what a lot of people think. I'm a positive thinker I have no problem with being a positive thinker. But do you really think you can wish things into existence? Do you really think if you wish hard enough, things will come true? Why not just change your focus? Stop wishing and start praying. Turn your eyes towards Jesus, and pray that He will help you in any given situation. Most of the time, He might not have your prayer right then, but He can show you a way to be a better person to live that Heaven on earth moment, just as I had, on that Wednesday afternoon.

CHAPTER 8 **The Dilemma**
Good n Plenty

Nehemiah 1:7 - We have sinned terribly by not obeying the commands, decrees, and regulations that you gave us through your servant Moses

One of the most difficult things I have seen as a Christian is approaching the stories about friends that have been hurt by churches. I know many people that have been in churches that didn't get it; they just let their flesh run the pulpit. I am not going to turn this book into a platform to judge churches. But you find out in several testimonies that churches hurt people. Not the church congregation, but the people running them.

For all those people that feel this way, please give a new church a second chance. I looked at finding a church the same as a college student finding a college. Look at the structure of the church and just make sure Bibles are open during the services. When my daughter was looking for a college, sometimes she would walk onto the campus and know if she was in the right place. One time we drove through the town and she said I just don't like it. I think that is very similar to finding a church.

My wife and I tried our home church Hosanna Lutheran in Lakeville, MN over 20 years ago. At the time we weren't looking to move and the church we were attending had a good children's program. But it wasn't moving either one of us from the lessons we were learning. It was just the same stories over and over. Then we attended Hosanna and a Pastor that is now in his own church on the west coast spoke. He lifted us both, and when we walked outside that day I said to my wife, "how are we going to leave our church".

We were really involved, we taught Sunday school, we prepared communion, and I occasionally mowed the property. But God pulled us in a different direction that day to a church that spoke from the Spirit. I didn't know it at the time, but it was there now that I look back on it. We joined weeks later and we have been members there since. I know God wanted us to be there, our kids have attended Power life and Catalyst and I love walking through those doors. Sometimes 4 to 5 times a week, and almost everything I attend invites the Holy Spirit in and welcomes His presence.

I don't think it is a coincidence that when Bill Boline started it, he always welcomed the Holy Spirit, and I think that is what draws people in. The key is the Holy Spirit and prayer. It is that easy, don't water it down, don't use fake shows or ideas, just invite the Holy Spirit in and see what happens. The staff is always praying and many of the members and prayer partners pray over the property weekly and each and every seat before the services.

That is where I started with my friend Rick that helped me and encouraged me to write this book. He was and so was his father completely burned by churches. He never really had a trust in churches he attended. Something always broke that trust that sent him back to his roots and his father's feelings about mistrust and the church. Rick has done a complete turnaround, he has slowly started to see the trust that Hosanna members have in the teachings. A different way of letting God know He is in control and not the church or its staff.

Rick and I started our story in an awesome way, totally brought on by the Holy Spirit. We met in a way that only the Holy Spirit could orchestrate. I was working with a company that was working in the credit industry, and the company was in the process of going public. Chris, the founder of the company, and I were working daily to get the company on the map. At the time I was 2 months out from the intercession on Feb 12th, and I was on fire for God and the stories of my faith were just flowing out of me. One time Chris and I prayed that someone would come along to help us with our marketing.

Chris and I sat down one day and we both agreed we needed to step up the marketing of the company. At the time this book wasn't in any part of my thoughts, I was just looking for a good marketing person. I had recently told my intercession prayer story to a friend and I had invited him to a Search Ministries event at a local Country Club. Search ministries is a local mission to help in our community to teach people about the love of Christ. As I was driving to the event, my friend called and said he couldn't make it. When I arrived I told Pat from Search Ministries that I wouldn't have a guest.

She sat me next to some other people. I ended up sitting right next to Rick. The speaker this morning was David Rohl that will be another story for another day. As I was sitting at the table little did I know I was placed next to the man that would be doing the illustrations for ths book. We had never met, so when he told me he was in marketing I asked him if he would take a quick look at our credit web site. This was on a Thursday morning, and I was leaving for s trip to San Antonio the next day. I told Chris back at the office about meeting Rick, and we were both excited. I told Chris we should pray that this was the right guy, and told him to have faith he would be the one to help us with our marketing. At this point I was heading out of town for vacation.

The week went by, I spent mornings walking the San Antonio river walk praying and one of my prayers that Rick would look at our web site and help us with the marketing of the business. Well when I returned the following Monday almost a week and a half after I first saw Rick. Chris asked me right away if I had heard from him, I said I hadn't. On Tuesday I got an email from Rick saying he had looked at our web site and he would like to meet with us. His email stated we needed help with our brand. Later I found out from Rick that he had pulled my card out from a place he wasn't even expecting to look at for a while. We met on the product and he had a new brand and look to our web site within days. He started working with us, and we began to have conversations about other things besides work. I ended up telling him about my intercession and a support group that met at noon called Prayer Transformation Ministries. Rick ended up coming to the group, and Chris started coming sometime after. Now Rick, Chris, and I attend it every Thursday.

The crazy part of this story is the fact that Rick and I have become really good friends. When I first suggested writing this book, he said he would do the illustrations. As I stated in the beginning of this chapter, Rick had fallen away from being involved in church. I looked at Rick and knew only he would know his heart, but I knew his heart was focused on Christ. When I look at people that have been burned by churches, it is sad to see them walk away and not get the teachings that help us deal with this world. I know I still judge people and make comments on how people live their lives, but I am trying daily to get better. I love churches that have doors open to all, and Rick has seen that in Hosanna. Go and visit the Brooklyn Tabernacle Church in New York if you want to hear or see the extreme of welcome to a church. Jim Cymbala will teach and show you how to say "Welcome."

I recently saw Jim, and I know writing this book and seeing everyone who welcomes anyone into their church is of God. Listen to Jim Cymbala on YouTube; he has 100's if not 1000's of stories of people walking into his church to escape the lives they were living. Many came and didn't feel anything, but some were blessed the very first time. The welcome is the way it should be, and we should be building up churches in our community.

Our pastor told an awesome story a few weeks back. There was a traditional church out on the west coast, and they were conducting a Sunday service. Everyone in their Sunday best, with no tie untied. There happened to be a college campus not too far away from this church and a student from the campus wanted to worship that day. He walked into the church with a cut off shirt, shorts and a pair of flip flops. He couldn't find a seat when he started up the center aisle. He walked all the way to the front and nothing to be found. He stopped and sat on the floor in the center aisle.

The pastor that day was just about ready to deliver his message when one of the elders of the church stated to walk towards the student. As he approached the pastor waited to see what would happen next, then the elder stopped and sat down next to him on the floor and welcomed the student. Then they both turned their eyes towards the pulpit and waited for the message to begin. I think the message was over at that point, enough said with just the actions of the elder.

That is how I hope your church welcomes its guests. No judging just love, the same love that God had for His guests. Come as you are to worship, I say a person coming to worship in rags, is better than a person coming in a $1,000.00 suit coming to judge. Jesus is the only judge that matters. Judge Judy will not be standing next to Jesus in Heaven. It is us and Him, no one else. That is why we shouldn't be the judge here on earth. That is a difficult task, when our entire culture is setup to judge each other.

I know there are many people that say they still find their peace and joy away from church. That is OK, but there is really a rare day that I attend church that I don't get inspired by the message. I know that can be true, but like the name of this book, "There is No Time Like Heaven" I feel being in those teaching and spiritual moments can be found in places of worship and in community. Again, that is me. If you find that in your kitchen, in your back yard, or walking your dog then by all means live that out. But, please be honest with yourself. Don't go because you are making excuses for not being there; just make an honest decision to worship in a way to edify God.

When you do go to worship I hope you see what the Holy Spirit brings to you. Sometimes during a message I will read a certain passage or I will get a certain message that's completely different from what's being spoken from the pulpit. I don't think that is against what is being spoken or who's giving the message I think is just God telling me what I need to hear that day. Many times I've been sitting in church or other places, and I literally felt that everybody could leave the room. There was one time during a seminar by Gabe Lyons I literally wanted to stand up in my chair and tell others they can go he was there just for me. During those times I know I was completely coherent to the Holy Spirit, and the Holy Spirit is really trying to teach me something in that moment.

Overall that's happened about six times in my time of being in service at Hosanna. But as it happened with Gabe Lyons, Tony Campello, and Jim Cymbala. During those moments, I could've literally been the only person in that auditorium. That's how powerful those moments can be, they grab you out of the blue. It is one of the neatest things I've ever seen in my walk with believing in Jesus. There are times I can't understand why that happens at that moment, but it just does, and it will happen to you at some point. One of the things I learned is don't go looking for it, don't force it. Just let it come to you, just like the day in my intercession on February 12, I never asked for that I just let it come to me. That is why when people say they can find their own way, I hope they aren't missing out on one of the Heaven On Earth Moments.

Recently I had lunch with my friend Merlyn, and we were talking about the time that we saw Tony Campello, and I almost flew out of my chair when he started talking something I was learning through prayer. We both just had a great time talking and reliving the moment, and the assurance that God brings to us every day that He is with us. I know it was the Holy Spirit, If this wasn't the Holy Spirit what is? As Jim Cymbala says, as God is my witness, strike me down now if these experiences didn't happen.

The title of this book came to me when I was talking with Rick, who helped me with this book. We are sitting in a restaurant talking about some of the things I've been through that week. I was telling him, that there is no time in Heaven. And it is really crazy that I came up with that name, OK the Holy Spirit came up with that name. In that the title of our book is perfect, because it truly is no time in Heaven. It is stated in the Bible, that there is no time in Heaven. It says in the Bible that in God's eyes, one day is like 1000 years in Heaven time. And I tried to explain to Rick, that this is something I agree is what we expect in Heaven. NO TIME! IN HEAVEN! God has shown me that everything happens simultaneously, this is a hard one to comprehend. Usually when I talk about this one, people think I'm off my rocker. Things happen simultaneously, this is hard to comprehend. It takes many conversations to share with people that this is true. Again I don't have all the answers and this is just what I think.

The cool thing is when you think about this answer, so many questions about creation and many questions about the way things happen on our lives. If everything happened simultaneous in Heaven, it really answers a lot of the questions that people have about afterlife. Some Christians think you go into a holding pattern right after you die in your resurrected body during the tribulation. That makes that statement true if everything happens at the same time, but again I'm not trying to convince you of this in my writing today. As I was explaining this to Rick that afternoon, I could see the confusion on his face I wanted this to be affirmed somehow someway. So later that day I looked for more Scripture, I just couldn't find it.

Fast forward to Friday night of that week, my son plays high school football at the time he was in ninth grade. I loved going to games, chance to unwind at the end of the week and watch some fun games. We attended all these high school games, and I was sitting there watching the game. At halftime I got up to get a hot chocolate. It was cold that night, and that Minnesota wind just blows right through you. When I turned around to get up I noticed that Scott and Merlyn were in the stands. They waved me over, they were trying to get my attention. Scott is a friend from coaching in sports and

Merlyn and I taught small groups at Powerlife at Hosanna, our youth program.

Merlyn and I had been on a retreat earlier that year, and we had some awesome conversations in our groups. The teenagers we had made some of our conversations extremely interesting. A few of those stories I will share in this book. Scott and I had many talks after our workouts at the local club.

They asked me to attend a speaking event the next morning. The speaker's name was Tony Campello, but I had never heard of him. I tried using a couple of excuses, but then I said I got nothing going on and I will see you in the morning. As I drove to Prince of Peace Church, I called Rick and told him what I was attending, he looked up Tony on the Internet while the seminar was in progress. I had not been back to this church since I attended my friend Jeff's funeral in the sanctuary. It was a surreal experience, knowing all the stuff I had been through since hearing of Jeff's death. I sat there listening to the first part of the program; Tony was extremely interesting and extremely funny. He was almost like Don Rickles doing standup for Christ. He showed the group that it's okay to laugh at church, he uses a lot of humor. Of course I already knew that so it was refreshing seeing someone have fun from the pulpit. I know that's okay with God. He gave us our gift to laugh, why wouldn't He enjoy us laughing. So at that point I continue to listen to Tony speak. Then out of the blue, he started talking about space and time travel. Traveling at the speed of light, and how time stops. He really makes sense when he explains it, and I suggest you look it up sometime and listen to him talk about these facts. But I could sense many people were confused on what he was talking about.

The main gist of it was if you travel the speed of light you do not age. It's a proven fact of science, I believe that with the Holy Spirit in Heaven there is no time, hence eternal life. During the time when he talked about this, I must've elbowed Merlyn 10 times. I was ready to jump out of my seat, I couldn't believe that these two men were planted at a football game to bring me to this point. God used this moment to bring together all these moments in my life. Maybe this had happened more before the day I got in the whirlpool, but I did not recognize it. I recognize it now though, and that is the power of the Holy Spirit. We had a short break before the second session; I told Merlyn I was writing a book. He thought it was really cool, and I told him the reason I kept elbowing him was that I had just talked about this "no time in Heaven" concept with my friend Rick two days earlier. He said, "you were about to jump out of your seat, it was fun to watch." The exact concept that Tony Campello had just talked to us about for 20 minutes, had the room spinning with confusion, but I understood.

I bet if you took a toll that morning out of the 500 to 700 people that were there, maybe 10 that would have gotten what he was talking about, or maybe just me. I'm not trying to put the glory back on me I'm just saying that thought came to my mind days before I was invited to go see this man. If that is not the Holy Spirit at work, then I don't know what is, and the funniest part of the story I named the book "There's No Time Like Heaven" months before I ever thought of this concept. But that's what community does, it brings Heaven to us through the Holy Spirit. That is the point I'm trying to make in this book there is no time like Heaven. God prepares a place for us, and the place is Heaven on earth. It's right in His own prayer.

It's hard to believe this concept, it's real, that is why I think it's important to be in community in the church. Seek others that are doing these types of things to see them. Again I'm not beating up the fact that you need to go to church please understand this, but I am stating the fact that I would've missed out on hundreds of times Heaven on earth without being in communion with others.

So if you are one of those people that say "I need to go to church. I get my church on the golf course, in front of the TV, or just spending time with my family." Do you know if you have the Holy Spirit in you? Have you invited Him into your soul. I respect that, I have a friend Dave and he is one of the most honest Christians I know, and he has been burned by churches several times over. I continually pray that he will be led by the Holy Spirit. Whether he might be at home or walking his dog. But I still pray God will fill him up in new ways, just like I have been. I just want to let you know that being in community is one of those places that I wouldn't trade for anything. As the advertising says, just do it!

CHAPTER 9 Planting Seeds
We are all farmers

Numbers 24:7 - Water will flow from their buckets; their offspring have all they need. Their king will be greater than Agag; their kingdom will be exalted.

Luke 8:5 – "The sower went out to sow his seed"

Planting seeds is something we do every day, and we don't even know it. I talked to someone just the other day that is planting seeds in my life, making me really think about my walk with God. This same person said this to me, "It seems like I am never in an area in my life where I plant seeds." I know this person is plating seeds with not only their words, but the way he lives his daily life. That is what's so amazing about living in the "As Earth as it is in Heaven," moments. We just have to expect the Holy Spirit will guide us in many moments, and He will. Recently I was at a football game and I was talking to a friend of mine. My son at the time was recovering from a broken arm and we were talking about some of my sons past injuries. The discussion turned to one of his injuries last fall when I was in Honduras. Next thing we know we are talking about the trip and why I went, and what was the purpose. I explained we did water projects and teaching in Honduras. We talked briefly about why I went on the trip and who also went from Lakeville. It was just one of those innocent conversations, but planting a small seed.

On another occasion I started with the same type of conversation. I went on to explain how Agua Viva was started on a porch in Lakeville, with a few Dads that wanted to make a difference. That led to me inviting him and one of his friends to an Agua Viva dinner. They haven't shown up at one yet, but the seed was planted. That is all God asked, the Holy Spirit does the rest. Yes we can keep on pushing them with more invitations, but let the seed do its work. There are tons of times in my life that have been just tiny cracks to let a message just drop in on someone's heart. It is like the Bible says, plant the seed and be patient for the harvest. There are seeds being planted all over the place, so the harvest can be plentiful. The battle is busting through all the rocks in our lives to see there is awesome soil below.

It is just amazing when you think of a seed; a friend of mine Barry was once at a golf tourney and was just having a normal non eventful afternoon. He sat down at a table with five or six guys, just having the normal golf chatter. Talking about the golf round, sports, and maybe a few seconds of family. Then out of the blue, a guy he barely knew started talking one on one with him about where he lived. The conversation changed to the schools and church his family attended. At that point it turned to my friend and what church he attended. He said it was a nice conversation, it didn't seem pressured it was just a nice talk. At that point he started talking about his walk with God, and how it had been up and down and all over. Then he asked my friend how he had felt his Faith walk was going. That was it, those few words. "How is your Faith walk doing" That was it!

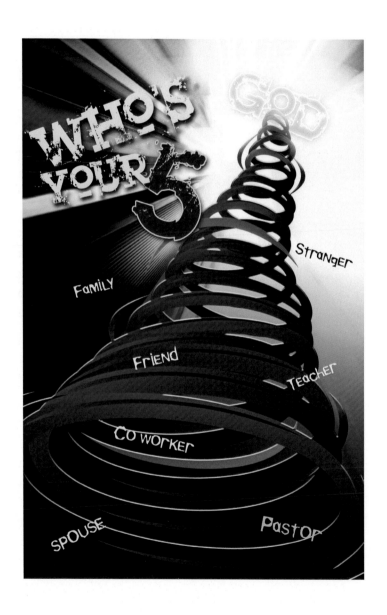

WHO'S YOUR 5

GOD

Stranger

Family

Friend

Teacher

Co worker

Spouse

Pastor

At the time, my friends walk wasn't out of control, he just knew in his heart he wasn't on the path God wanted it to be. He knew in his heart he needed to see that God had more for him. These are the moments that I talked about earlier in my story. It wasn't that he was off the team, he was on the sidelines and God didn't have him on the field. That night he went home and started thinking about what he meant, maybe the guy he was talking with didn't even know he was planting the seed, or maybe he did. But I am sure he had no clue how big the harvest would be from that situation. But he did a big matzo ball seed. My friend thought about it more and more as the week went on, and to this day he said it was the deciding moment that put him back on the field was that night with that conversation. OK, that is one seed that changed my friends life. Now what are seeds that have been planted in your life?

These moments when you get into a discussion like this are Heaven on Earth moments. Many times I have no clue where the words came from in the conversation. Many times I just let the conversation flow, and at no point do I have a agenda. Right after I had my intercession on February 12, I wanted to tell everyone about it, at first I was going at it the wrong way. I would bring it up, and try to slam it at people. Then I learned over time, it wasn't about me, it was about what God decided to do that morning. I wasn't asking or looking to be that person that He spoke through. So I decided to let God lead the conversations, It is still hard to this day to explain it without having my head explode with excitement. Ok, planting seeds is telling stories, sharing with a bridge of trust. I never thought of myself as being great at witnessing, but I do have a good sense of humor and I'm also really good at telling stories. That is the way I plant seeds, one story at a time.

Now stop and write down 5 people who have planted seeds in your life. 5 important people that helped you get to where you are with your relationship with God. Not people from today, go deeper. Look for people that changed your foundation. People you trust and have planted trustworthy thoughts that helped you understand the love of God. I can't believe how deep this made me think of my past. It was crazy; I started contacting the people that helped me get to where I am today. I first and foremast included my parents, they built the foundation of the rock I stand on today. We went to church weekly and it was a priority in our house. I liked hanging out there; it was a place to have fun. I really became a Christian when I was 23, in my senior year at college. Although I didn't really realize it at the time, I had many people that planted seeds to get me to the cross.

I wrote down 5 people that influenced me up to that point. It was right around the time I met my wife Keri. I had said the prayer before that point, but that was the one that stuck. The people besides my parents, were youth pastors and leaders. My grandma Mini and her singing and watching Billy Graham were defiantly in the mix. That was really one of the coolest things about writing about this in this chapter. One aspect was digging deep to find who planted the seeds in my life. It required picking up the phone and talking to some friends from over 30 years ago. Just crazy, and the connections we all forget about, and not praising God for putting them in our path. In my journey to find my 5 seeds I looked up a high school buddy from 30 plus years back. I couldn't remember a couple of the youth mentors I had, so I knew Bob would know. I looked up Bob, and gave him a call. Bob is now a pastor in the northern suburbs of Minneapolis, and it was great to see him. We met for coffee, and talked about these two guys that really helped as young high school kids. They were probably in a place in their faith walk where I am now, and helping our youth. I not only look back on those 5 seeds, but then I think of the 5 that brought each one of them to the cross. That is 25 people from a generation that helped and ministered each one of them. That is what I think will happen in Heaven, I think a person will come up to me from 5 generations removed for my Honduras trip and thank me for my service. I truly think that is what Heaven will be like, telling stories of how we helped build the kingdom. I think that is what is meant by the singing in Heaven, it will be the stories of building the Lord's Kingdom.

When I sat down Bob and I had coffee and we talked about some of the stories and things we did as children. We both realized that was faith-based. Even though we did a lot of boneheaded dumb things in high school, we still had that faith that we could turn to even when we weren't 100% about God. But it was neat because we talked about when we ended up at a couple of those youth directors' apartments some nights. We watched hockey and basketball on TV, then one of the leaders, John, would share a story or read a Bible verse to us. We didn't realize at the time, he was a planting a seed in each one of us. And I think that's what is really missing in our youth today. Sure they do dumb things and make terrible decisions, but the important thing is that they can stand on a rock and they can turn to Him whenever they need it.

Look at the following diagram:

Notice how the seeds just multiply so fast, some of them may take a lifetime.

One of things I like to think about, is the different people that are doing really cool ministry around the world. Take a look at Agua Viva. The next thing I like to think about is the 25 people who have helped you grow more spiritually. Think hard and think of 25 seeds or 25 people that have planted seeds in your life to help you learn more and live in community. Think of the way you bought this book, did someone give it to you or did someone do something in your life that brought you closer to a relationship with God. Planting a seed is just living your life the way it is meant to be, just living with a What Would Jesus Do mentality. That is something I try to do, I don't have to tell people that I am a believer; I want them to see it in me. By the way I live it out, filling up my buckets, to overflow. Not proving anything to anyone, just being the person God wants me to be. Using the gifts He has blessed me with that is what planting a seed is all about. If you planted 5 goodness seeds about the glory of God over your lifetime in 5 people, do you know what that would mean? That is like the movie "Pay it forward." The seeds just pass on as people grow to be better people, moving closer to God. If 5 people planted 5 seeds in their lifetimes and so on, the numbers add up very quickly. 5 become, 25, and 25 becomes, 125, and 125 becomes 625 and so on. As shown in the diagram 12 deep touches over 48 million people. In Luke chapter 8 it talks about how we plant our seeds. How some are planted on the rocky road and never get to the soil. They are then eaten up by passing birds. Then some seeds fell on rocky soil, they grew but withered away from no moisture. Then seeds fell upon the thorns and where choked away. Lastly the seed that fell in fertile soil and grew up to produce a 100 fold, that is when it gets exciting.

Now planting a seed on a cement area is never going to grow, hardened hearts are the most difficult to penetrate. But, we can drop the seed on the cement and how a tiny wind comes along, someone else planting a seed and pushes it to the tiniest of cracks or a radical wind that blows into fertile soil. That is how this whole process works; planting seeds isn't hard if you just plant them in people that trust you. I think many times we need to build a line of trust first, and then plant the seeds. I like what Gabe Lyons says, "I have been witnessing to my neighbor for 7 years, and he doesn't even know it." Planting seeds are in everyone's testimonies; you hear how people planted just tiny thoughts in others. When we live it, it can be a wonderful thing, living it without judging others. Just dropping seeds all over the place.

That is the fertile soil part, that is the friendship and trust you build up. The more they trust you the more the soil is ready. That is why we don't have to be pushing our views right down other's throats right when we meet them, just be their friend. It is the same process you go through when you get to know Jesus. It isn't the moment you meet Him that you just instantly know Him. I will talk about that later in this book. Just nurture the friendship and watch what will happen. If I have a friend that is constantly battling me with his views and his concerns. Every time we discuss something he tries to change my point of view. That is someone I guarantee I won't be spending any time around. Discussions are good, views are good, but people don't want to be pushed into decisions. They want to learn where the facts are coming from, and what their motivation is.

We need to bridge the gap and build trust. That is the way we plant seeds in people. It is how we communicate with others that is the key. I approach friends with what they like and how they live their lives. Too many times we approach others with just our concerns on our minds. This is an area I am really working on, I need to zip the lip and let others tell me what is on their mind. There are two ways to plant seeds, one is to plant it with someone we trust and the other is to just throw something out there to someone we might not even know. Many of the seed planting stories I have heard have been both. I just heard one at a meeting for an upcoming trip to Honduras. Chris one of the groups going on the next trip gave his testimony recently. He had a really tough road; he was really spiraling downward when he was in a bad accident. He was laying in the hospital days later, completely broken both physically and mentally.

He didn't trust anyone at the time, and out of the blue a family visiting the guy he shared his hospital room with just stopped and asked him if he needed prayer—no connection, just prayer. This act of kindness changed him. It didn't change him instantly. But to this day that is the day he started trusting people. He thought of how kind that thought was, he was at a point in his life where most of the Christians he had met where hypocrites. People that understand that God's plan is bigger than their plan, don't want anything but to just pray. This story of a seed planted firmly in his heart from a complete stranger. How cool is that? I bet everyone one of us has several people planting seeds non-stop around us everyday.

Then there is me, I was once listening to the radio and a man said, "It takes more of God's power to save an unbelieving sole than it did to create the entire universe." Wow, when I heard that I almost ran off the road. But that sank in so deep, I thought about it for days. Just how important it is to keep being nice to one another and creating conversations that build a ton of trust. That is how we get to one another to create the circles of trust that will change this world. One person, and one soul at a time. That is why I just like talking with people and sharing our struggles together. We all struggle, and we are all going to face tough moments in our lives. It is how we react to those situations and who we trust at those tough moments. Right now think if you were stranded in the middle of the night and you needed to call for help. Who are your trusted friends, who would you count to come. I mean leave whatever they are doing and come help you? Can You think of 10 people? I can think of way more than that, and that is a good feeling to have, especially in tough situations.

Right there is a community of people, people banding together to solve a problem that we can't solve on our own. When I meet with the group at Hosanna on Thursday mornings and we pray, we can all feel the trust we have in the Holy Spirit to answer our prayers. I still think about that at least once a day. But I also keep telling others about that statement, planting more seeds so others can move them forward. Seed planting is good, the harvest is out there. You also have to plant in good soil. So you might be tilling soil some days and planting others. Different seasons, there is also a time when the soil needs to just lay dormant and rest. So keep that in mind, we need to stop and smell the roses every so often.

There are two kinds of seeds, good and bad. We all have weeds in our garden; we need to be pulling the bad seeds we get daily and keeping our garden clean of junk and distractions. Be careful of the bad seeds; always be on the lookout for things that people say Christian or Non-Christian that plant a bad seed. Yes, they can come from anyone. Every day we are being attacked and we have to watch out for those falling bad seeds. Let the good seeds pour into your heart; I get them all day long. Radio, Stories, Bible, and YES the most from friends.

Some of the testimonies I have heard will never leave my heart, ever! I have been a prayer partner for the Bethel College mission trips to Honduras, I once went on. Each spring Jay takes a group of students down there, and I have been a prayer partner. The best part is watching this spring mission trip to Honduras, and the seeds that are being planted through the Bethel College students. The trips started years ago when they couldn't even get enough kids to go, but now there's a 30+ waiting list. Kids can't wait to get down there. Seeds are being planted all of the time by the experiences on these trips, and the changes the students go through living out the classroom in a real-world situation.

These are the ripples that are sent out each and every day. I love talking about the ripples and how these go out in all different directions. The same as I talked about one planting seeds, straight back at you a lot of times, and they come back to bless us all over again and again throughout our lives. But sometimes ripples stop when they get out too far, and sometimes they keep going for eternity. These ripples go out in every direction, and every time I see stories or situations that touch somebody, and then the touch of somebody else, it just keeps going and going almost like a video going viral. It is so awesome to see somebody touch another life with God's love, and that love being taught or passed on to someone else.

Just take for instance, me getting out of that whirlpool on February 12th. I had no idea the ripples that would go out in thousands of different directions. I had friends that asked me to several different things at church, my friend Andy had been asking me for months to attend our Thursday morning prayer time at Hosanna. I thought about it, and I wasn't sure I'd ever go. The next week after the intercession I went. And I can't even tell you how many ripples have broken out from that, and how many things that touched my life.

From that prayer time, I first got the idea to put together the forms for the unemployed in Financial Peace class. I know if I wasn't in prayer force I would've never brought that idea to anyone at the church. Because I was there and had a platform to explain the story of how people were finding jobs in this church class. I brought it up Thursday morning, then Sharon brought up the fact that she was touched also, to start the same thing, and she had a heart for the unemployed. But this all started years back when the seed was planted by Colleen and Mike, who started the intercessory prayer team. Colleen came up with the idea to start the I-TEAMS to pray for other things around church.

So that was a ripple, that really started way out and it's Colleen and Mike that were praying for the I-TEAMS. Pat, our care ministry leader, was praying for the Career Connections to expand from just Tuesday nights when we provide a meal and other things at our church. Years later, I was driving down the road and knew God told me to put the forms together for those unemployed at Financial Peace. These were those ripples just expanding out, so I brought it up on a Thursday morning. Sharon was there and started to get emotional about the unemployed. Then we met with Andy, a mutual friend, to gain a praying force behind it. Now we have people praying for the I-TEAMS, people praying for the expansion of this from Tuesday night, and all these ripples came together.

This is when it got exciting, when the people from our church stepped up and joined our team—another seven of us that run these career connections meetings the first Saturday of every month, and those ripples go up forever. There are so many stories of people that got a job through prayer and hard work, that touched others and now those stories are just sending out in all different directions. That is when it gets really really really cool. Everyone came together, and now these ripples are just speeding out in all different directions. Every month we have some come in and give a testimony of the job they found and how they were touched by the process.

Those stories touched the people that were there, and those ripples shot out in all different directions. I truly believe this is what God wants for His kingdom, thy kingdom come it will be done on earth as in Heaven. This is what He really truly wanted with these ripples just going all throughout the community hands and feet doing it. But now I really like to think of it a different way. How about the ripples that were started in Pat's life, in Mike's life, in Colleen's life, and in any life. The seeds were planted by five people as stated earlier in this chapter. Now really look at the ripples, they spread out all the way back to His people who believe this community concept, and believing that this is all how God wants to see His kingdom. This is where the beauty really shines, when these ripples go out in all directions creating a better place to make this Heaven on earth.

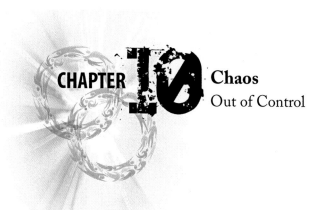

CHAPTER 10 Chaos
Out of Control

Genesis 42:12 - Yes, you are!" Joseph insisted. "You have come to see how vulnerable our land has become."

Trying to understand the chaos is the hard thing. When I look back at the reason I'm writing this book, I think it's to cut through the chaos. I look back at my life before February 12th, and the changes I made in prayer and understanding that the Holy Spirit is real. I just think that people need to realize, they can do more and they can be more involved without really doing that much more in their lives. Chaos can be sin and it can also be a blessing. The chaos of this sinful world is always chaos; yes we can try to say that we can make it less confusing and crazy. But, it won't happen, everyone is stuck inside a pinball machine just bouncing from place to place. These two pinball machines are illustrated below. One side is the goal is about ME the other side is about GOD and His ultimate plan. Do we want to have a story that is all about "ME", or a story that can be told for eternal life, and God's plan?

See the life illustration (like a pinball machine):

We are constantly trying to stay healthy, happy and ahead of the Jones. We are constantly connecting with others and trying to keep up with others. And if you have kids, forget about it, we are going all the time. Weeks are just flying by, our heads are spinning. If it's flying by, isn't it better to let it fly by with a goal and to connect with others and at least make some or most of our time geared with words helping others. Connecting the dots starts from your earlier days, the real circles in my life started 50 years ago. I have been creating them every day of my life. Childhood circles, young adult circles, college circles, and Christian and non-Christian adult circles. But, until February 12, 2011 the circles have never made sense, but there are still many days it doesn't. Yes, they were friends and friendships that I will have for a lifetime, but did they have full meaning? When we first hear the gospel, we have questions. At least I did, wondering how I would have to change the way I live. One thing I have learned is that the gospel is right from God. It is the difference between the Old Testament and the New Testament, Old is under a law, and the new is under the cross and the grace of God. In simple terms, the old was a bunch of rules and the new is a promise that Jesus made, if we believe in our hearts we are covered by His blood that He shed on the cross. If Jesus came back and changed the New Testament message and said what He did on the cross didn't count anymore what would happen? It would mean there wouldn't be one person destined for Heaven, we are all sinners and we all fall short.

Learning and accepting of the Gospel is a little like Neal Armstrong's first step on the moon. It is one small step for you, but a giant step for your eternal life. I am not in any way saying the message of Jesus dying on the cross isn't the most important thing that ever happened to mankind. But I am saying it is one small step to many small and large steps ahead. When you hear the gospel, it is like a master owner calling for his dog, he yells and the dog can either come or run away. It is that simple, when you hear a story or the gospel, you are being called by God. You can either come to it or run away from it. I heard once that Americans hear the Gospel at least 7 times in their lifetime. So we all have many chances to come back to our master. It is as simple as Romans 10:9, If you declare with your mouth, "Jesus is Lord," and believe in your heart that God raised Him from the dead, you will be saved.

That is where the journey begins, from that point on, and like me it might not truly hit you for years. I think that is one of the most important things about faith, we have to be patient with God. That is one thing I have never had, patience. My Dad says I am so impatient, but I am learning to wait on God. I have seen so many times when people get way ahead of God. That is why we need to wait on Him, keep praying and waiting for answers. And understand that everyone is always at a different place in their faith journey, I am trying to be patient with others too.

When I went to the intercession and had the meeting with Jay and started organizing different fundraising events, I was completely out of control. There were times I was way ahead of God. It was fine but there were some decisions I made that with experience now I would have slowed down and prayed about. When I first met with all four of of the guys from Agua Viva, I was talking a mile a minute and wanted to bring in as much money to make as many water systems as we could. Then sitting there at a local restaurant they slid a book across the table. The name of the book was, "When Helping Hurts." I down loaded the book and listened to it right away. After listening to the book, I realized how we should help others, and minister to others. It's not about just throwing stuff and money at others; it is about relationships and the ability to have a bond of trust. I saw that when I went to Honduras later that year.

Once you take this first small step, really the biggest one you will ever take, but still small. Before that it just seemed like ways to connect in this crazy world. Like the hamster on the treadmill, like my friend Chris says. At first in my journey it was connections with some spiritual connections, but most of them where for my glory. It was always about me, and a lot of the times it still is all about me. I am trying to change that in my life, but it isn't easy, baby steps. All my glory, never really for anything or anyone else. I have learned to pray and ask the Holy Spirit to help me through the "ME" factor. The praying part is the part that I have really understood the most. The dots started to connect, as you see in the illustration.

The dots just started. The dots are each individual circle. The circles are not created unless you are provoked and you take action for each one of them. There are hundreds of times I connect with someone and I see the Spirit working through that connection. I understand the power of the Holy Spirit in these connections. There are four to five things going on in my life right now that have sprung out of the intercession on Feb. 12th Each one of those situations are about glorifying God through service. Now service is a tough one, I do know one thing that we cannot go to true service without sanctification.

The Spirit had me take action that morning, not only to pray for my good friend Mike, but also to look at God and His presence through prayer. When I sat at that table and hearing the words, "We will not leave here until God speaks through one of us." I was still doubtful; I was thinking this will take all day. This won't happen in front of my eyes, and it didn't because it happened right inside of my soul. I realized that day, that we have to trust God with everything. All His to go under His power. It doesn't mean you can just sit back and wait for something to happen; you have to still put effort in and let Him guide you. You still have to work at improving yourself and working towards goals. Like writing this book, it takes my worldly body to push myself to take time to write. Once I started writing, the words just flowed from my thoughts, I know that is the Holy Spirit working through me.

I know the day the Holy Spirit rained down on me for that first prayer intercession. I was not cleaned out of some of the sins that where heavy on my heart. But, since then I have learned you need a clean heart to listen and to work through your soul. We just need to ask with a completely open heart. But when we ask we need to be cleaned out and ready to invite the Spirit within our hearts to be completely ready. It says in *Luke 11:33-36 - [33]"No one after lighting a lamp puts it in a cellar or under a basket, but on a stand, so that those who enter may see the light. [34]Your eye is the lamp of your body. When your eye is healthy, your whole body is full of light, but when it is bad, your body is full of darkness. [35]Therefore be careful lest the light in you be darkness. [36]If then your whole body is full of light, having no part dark, it will be wholly bright, as when a lamp with its rays gives you light."*

I have just seen this over and over; we cannot enter the Holy of Holies without bringing our sins to the cross. We cannot have anything between us and the path to God which is through the Holy Spirit. That is why it is so important to find the way to clean your heart is your personal way of cleansing your heart. The blood of Jesus does make that connection, but we need to get anything off our mind that is distracting us in anyway. Some of it is prayer, some it is worship music; it just needs to put your heart in the place you know you are clear from distractions and thoughts that will keep you from communicating with the Holy Spirit.

Either we are in control, or the Spirit that created the World is in control. I try to center things always looking for ways to see Christ in everything. I am now looking at my learning as part of my spiritual journey. Look for good in these situations. As I was sitting at my computer one evening, I happened to go on to our church website and looked at their "I Lift" conference. I had heard many times about the conference, but wasn't sure if it was for me at this point in my journey. I had been really busy at work, and I was scheduled to travel to Kansas City to do a presentation. I also had a planning meeting on Monday, so I knew I couldn't attend. God had different plans. As I was sitting there doing some work, I started to think about this lift Conference and should I attend. I could feel a nudging on my heart to register. The key is to listen to the Holy Spirit when you are in the chaos, and try to figure out ways to slow it down. So I did, and I knew I shouldn't do the amount of work I had that week. Well the next week I attended, Gabe Lyons, who was the main speaker. When he was about 10 minutes into his talk I was ready to just tell everyone in the room to leave. He was here just for me, he didn't need to speak to anyone else. That is the way I sense that the Holy Spirit is speaking to me through others and Scripture. The moment you can just boot everyone else out of the room, that is the moment for me. This has happened about 15 times since the intercession, and every time it has happened I just had no clue it was coming. I think if I had begged for it nothing would happen. I am no expert on the Holy Spirit. That day I wasn't looking for anything, matter of fact, I was the opposite. Get me out of this room. How am I ever going to get out of here? That is the most difficult part of the Holy Spirit and how He uses people. I am not versed in the Bible, I don't preach, but He wants to use me right now and I am saying yes. You won't find me hanging out with super religious people 24/7 or you won't find me hanging out with non-believers 24/7. But I do hang out with both, and I think that is what God wants us to do.

One of the connection stories that continues to come to my mind is when I was trying to contact Jay through email. At the prayer force I was so full of the Holy Spirit I was just crazy for the Holy Spirit. I was emailing people trying to figure out what Jay's email was. My friend Jenny had Jay's email and I was able to email him. Jay responded to it the very next day. When I saw that I sent a message to Jim and Jenny to get Jay's email address. I remember telling my wife in the kitchen that I would write down anything connected that made sense.

This gets to be hard to tell without getting confused. The Spirit is above all knowledge *Ephesians 3:19 - "and to know the love of Christ which surpasses knowledge, that you may be filled up to all the fullness of God."* This is what is talked about to be filled with the Holy Spirit. So back to my story about contacting Jenny to find Jay's email address. At that time Dawn was a friend from prayer force and we were praying for her husband that Thursday morning. Her husband was looking for a job in human resources. When I sent back Jay's email I saw that Jenny was working in Human Resources at a big Minnesota company. I knew this was God and the Holy Spirit affirming to me that I had made the right connection. I was able to connect Dawn with Jenny. Jenny talked to Dawn's husband about possibly working for her company in Human Resources. He ended up not getting the job, but he did end up gaining confidence to get a job with another company. It was really cool to see how the Holy Spirit was working. What makes it more crazy is that Jenny had moved into Dawn's neighborhood earlier that month. I found out later they ended up living two houses apart. Jenny and Dawn both love dogs. And to this day they still walk their dogs together, and have become good friends.

If you expand out the circles, and the Holy Spirit continues to touch through each one of these stories they are definitely connected together. I still see Dawn's husband around church, and now we have become friends. If the circles expand out if you see in the diagram, the Holy Spirit works through each one of us, and Dawn's husband is no exception. He was really struggling at one point in trying to find a job, he was sitting in the parking lot of a local restaurant, he was waiting to meet a friend. As he sat there, he prayed that God would show him a sign that he would find a job and things to be okay. As he lifted his head up from the steering wheel, the lead pastor from our church, Bill, walked right in front of his car. The next day he got a job. I believe this is how the Holy Spirit works, connecting all the different things that happen in each one of our lives. I see it happen over and over and over.

That is what's so hard about living in the chaos, we are constantly bouncing around from place to place. This is where I think if we just use the Holy Spirit to help live our daily lives, we can make things like this happen every day. That is why when I hear people explain the gospel and how you can change your life, I think the point they make is great. But I think really people miss the fact that we are still to be in the chaos. That each and every day our lives are upside down, and that is where we need to ask the Holy Spirit to interact in our lives to help us manage them. You saw earlier in this book how the the buckets in each one of our compartments of life need to be managed and improved upon. That is really where I think this all changes, the gospel is about coming to Christ and accept Him as your Savior, but it's also about taking baby steps. When we accept the gospel, we cannot just instantly change, yes really change in the inside out but it will take time. Just like putting together your kids' toys on Christmas Day. You have no idea how to put that thing together before you open the instructions. So how can we expect people to change when they have just heard the gospel, when they haven't read one page of the instruction manual. It's about not only growing in what the Bible teaches us but what others teach us.

Now figuring out where the Holy Spirit will talk to us is one thing, I think He speaks to us in many different ways. This is my opinion, I just think that we need to be looking for the Holy Spirit in everything were doing. I studied Acts a little bit, and Jim Cymbala never talked about the Holy Spirit in many of his messages. But I believe we find the Holy Spirit in reading the Bible, listening to others, and looking for it in many different avenues. I heard this once, I can't remember where I heard it, but here's how it looks.

Holy Spirirt:

1. Scripture
2. Messages
3. Stories
4. Events (could include movies, songs, and readings)
5. Dreams

I really wasn't sure about the part of the dreams, but in the chaos of being on the trip to Honduras last November.

I did get up early one morning and I was writing again. I got tired and I went back to sleep for a few minutes. I had a dream about one of the Hondurans name Adolfo. In the dream he had a concern about something he wanted to pray for in the group. It was funny because the group was back at Gustavo's house, but we never traveled to Gustavo's house. I was confused when I woke up, but I thought about it all day. I was going through some emotions after I had experienced one of the grossest, cockroach-infested bathrooms I had ever seen. I met up with a blind man on the side of the road. I'd been feeling sorry for myself about the bathroom situation in Honduras, but once I had met this 75-year-old blind man, I wondered how I could be feeling sorry for myself, when this man had lived here his entire life. He was a very nice man, we exchanged welcomes. When I saw Jay I broke down in tears, thinking about this blind man. And I told Jay how I had felt sorry for myself, until I met this man who lives in these conditions without sight.

I wasn't going to tell Jay about my dream earlier that day, but the moment and the emotions let it out. It was real similar to my intercession, I didn't believe my dream could be real, that the Holy Spirit could speak to me through a dream. So I told Jay about what I experienced I told him that I had a dream about a Adolfo, and that he wanted to pray for something. But in the dream we are back at Gustavo's house, so how could that be happening, so there's no way he could ask for that prayer request. Well Jay, let's go ask him, so we walked up to him and asked Adolfo if he had a prayer request. He started to get emotional, and explained to us that he really wanted us to pray for his son. His son was 14 years old was having some trouble in school, his son was also having a tough time relating to his mother. This was funny, I had a son at home was 14 and was having some trouble in school and was also having a hard time relating to his mother. So the three of us prayed together, praying for my son 3000 miles north in America, and Adolfo son right there in Honduras. This was the first time I'd ever experienced a dream that was sent by the Holy Spirit. As time has passed both his sons are doing better and my son is doing better. Recently I saw my son hug my wife; they are getting along great, not perfect, but better than before.

So it is amazing in the chaos sometimes, all the Holy Spirit shows us things. Not only in our lives but in others, we had to be constantly looking for these signs. I know it's frustrating every day getting up and trying to keep this in front of us, but I think it all starts with praying in keeping God in front. That is where we need to call the Holy Spirit each and every day. I'm not a very motivated person when it comes to writing or doing things on paper, so the chaos of writing this book was very difficult. There were days when I just didn't want to write, and there were days when I didn't feel like writing. I would use a lot of time to call on the Holy Spirit to help me get through it. I look back on this three-year journey and think of how it showed me so many things in my life. I believe that God took me out of the whirlpool that day on February 12, 2011. That's when He took me out of my comfort zone. He took me outside the gate. He wanted to show me the miracle of the Holy Spirit, the same Holy Spirit that fell down on thousands of people in Acts 4 in the New Testament.

Life in Christ is great but people after realized it can be better when you totally let your life be lifted by the Spirit. I saw hundreds of times throughout this journey. The neat thing is whenever I'd listen to a book on tape, to stories very similar to mine. Being provoked by the Holy Spirit is something we all go through we just need to recognize it. I'm not sure what

God has for me after this book journey. I have to listen to Him and grow in the process of the Spirit-filled submission. God has a plan. He is all knowing but He's also called each of us to carry out that plan. In Jeremiah it talks about the fact that He knew my plan before I was born. I saw Francis Chan give a talk on that reality. It gave me huge confidence when I realized that God knew my plan before I was in my mother's womb. I could be called upon to just do things in my local church or I could be called upon to do things somewhere else where God wants me to be, I just need to listen and find out where that is. When we step out into the chaos each and every day, it's so hard to find the Holy Spirit in it. Each and every day we get up with all these different agendas trying to stay ahead. As my friend Chris said we are constantly on the treadmill. One of the craziest moments of my life was when I stepped off the plane and into customs in Atlanta on my way back from Honduras. Here I'd spent a week with no running water no electricity and nothing really of any electronic value. It was calm and quiet at night, there were nights we just sat around the fire and sang songs. Unheard of in my family, electronics rule the world.

As we stepped off the plane, I remember standing at customs, and it said don't turn your cell phone on. Well, what do you think I did, I turned my phone on for the text messages. I went from this calm person five minutes earlier, praying with my friend John on the airplane to this crazy moment standing there watching my messages load onto my phone. Then I started to read the messages one by one. First there were customers that didn't get their product, then there was one for my dad saying my mom had hip surgery, and then there is one for my wife saying my son broke his foot. Right there, in a line in Atlanta Georgia I went from quiet subdued to calling on the Holy Spirit during this crazy chaotic moment. It made me realize how much chaos we really live in and how out-of-control we all are but it also made me realize that's the world we live in. In the chaos we need to see the Holy Spirit. I know a lot of people have gone through this type of situation, especially when you are returning from a mission trip or a nice long vacation. All I know is I have to take my mind back to that moment and look for the Holy Spirit in every situation. And I need to pray that the chaos will not overtake me, because life without chaos is impossible in the United States. Well maybe not impossible, maybe if you moved to a farm or small town, but even there you can't get rid of electronics. So the real key is to search for the Holy Spirit throughout the chaos.

And I think the best way to get around the chaos, is to find groups of people who are willing to pray together outside the chaos. At church we have a Thursday morning group called Prayer Force. The Holy Spirit shows up every week, what we experience in that room is nothing short of amazing. There've been times we prayed for just one person to be healed. And there are times we prayed for a pastor to give a message of concern. Each one of the situations we asked the Holy Spirit to come in and we look at the situation cut to the chaos of the situation. That is where you really see how the Holy Spirit as He works in a community of prayer. The one area of prayer in my life I need to work on is my home prayer praying with my wife. But in community I have seen it over and over that the Holy Spirit just rains down on groups. Each situation and really shows us how we need to pray for answers to our prayers. When I look back and going from the intercession on February 12th, not really knowing what was, joining up where I am today. Externally I haven't changed a ton, but internally I have changed enormously. What I try to do now is just love other people, be nice to them and learn from others while trying to cut through the chaos of everyday life.

At the end of the day if you organize your life around what God teaches us, it will come out that we will be rewarded. I am not saying that doing good deeds will ensure it all comes out in the end, I am just saying if we stay inside the boundaries of putting God first we will be rewarded. This is the Heaven on earth that I have talked about, it keeps us in the flock where our Shepard can watch over us each and every day. Just like the Ten Commandments aren't for us to be struck down by God to follow, they are more like boundaries. Shea, the head of our youth department at church was speaking the other day, and made a great point. When you look at the Ten Commandments, they are like boundaries. Some use the example of a tsunami or a giant wave, that goes into an area and causes complete havoc. When the waters silent or calm, in doing what it's supposed to do with in its boundaries, that is when things are beautiful and calm. But when some big storm comes, like a storm surge in a hurricane or a tsunami in the water goes outside its boundaries that causes complete destruction. We've seen this both in the US and in other countries in the past few years. The water causes unbelievable destruction, it takes years to repair. As she explained the Ten Commandments, they are boundaries and we go outside the boundaries it can cause havoc.

When I look back in my life, at the time that I was really thinking it was all about me and all about doing it my way. I went outside of these boundaries, and caused havoc. That is exactly what Shea is talking about, God's rules in God's commandments are for us to obey and stay within those boundaries. And sometimes it's really difficult in the chaos, to stay within those boundaries and to live our lives the way we should be living them. That is why you need to do more for God's plan and less for our plan and things will work out. I believe growing, through the word and through God's teachings is one of the main ways to stay within these boundaries. However interesting the boundaries, if we don't know what the boundaries are that is what really keeps us motivated and coming back to learn more about God. The cool thing I've learned in my journey is that there are many many many disciples and people throughout the Bible that constantly went outside the boundaries but it caused havoc in their lives. You see this in David's life, you see this in Matthew's life, and Peter's life and these were some of the most important people and stories in the Bible. They all went outside of God's walls, but they also all learned that they couldn't do it on their own.

John 3:30 says, "He must increase, but I must decrease." I think when I look at this verse, it really makes me realize how it had to be more about Him and less about me. Really focusing in on God's plan, and that's the most difficult thing in the chaos. Every day just gets crazier and crazier in this world we live in, it gets faster and faster, technology just makes us fly from day-to-day. And as you get older the weeks go faster, I always knew that was coming because my mom and dad always stressed that. But in the chaos, if we include God in the community of others we really start to see how we can grow. I believe this growth is worth the effort, learning more and more about how He wants us to live in learning to manage the chaos. So today, find that few minutes to stop and learn a verse, or find a few minutes to text a friend a Bible verse. Use technology as a benefit to learn more about God, there are hundreds and hundreds of videos on YouTube that can teach us God's ways, and the way we should live our lives. Some of the speakers I listen to on YouTube, I listen while working out in the morning, and it motivates me in each area of my life. It helps to cut through the chaos, and control the balance that sanctification needs.

One thing I have learned, is that the more I learn the more I want to learn. I love also, taking stories of the Bible and making them extremely simple. I think that's one of the biggest messages that I have from my life, is just making this gospel as simple as possible. Just like when Jesus asked Matthew, to drop everything and follow Him. He didn't say drop everything and accept His life, and give up all the things he was doing and follow Him. Jesus just said follow Him, that simple. That is my goal to make this as simple as possible, sure they'll be others that want to make it more complicated, and that's fine. I just know the Lord wants me to send a message of how simple this gospel really is, I don't live my life perfect and I will never claim to live my life in a perfect manner. I still am messed up all the time, I'm still tempted every day, and I still give in to temptation. But I do know one thing, by what I've learned there are hundreds of people in the Bible that given the temptation, but the most amazing thing is that God always showed His mercy toward His people. That is what I think is the most amazing thing about God, I still have a hard time forgiving others and being obedient to God. But I know He forgives me and shows me mercy. So every day in this chaotic life we live in, I just know my God will show me mercy.

And when I ask Him to intercede in situations that need interceding in prayer I know He will be there for me. Sometimes the prayers aren't answered right away but other times they are and that's what I think is really cool about being a believer. Today all of my life is no different than any other, getting work done in balancing the chaos but I will look at where God wants me today and how He wants me to live my life. And through teaching, and understanding I will learn more about how I'm supposed to live. I'll be one step closer to cutting to the chaos but yet living Heaven on earth. As the book title "There is No Time Like Heaven," I truly believe if we can battle through the chaos and find a place for Jesus in our lives Heaven can be part of earth just like the Lord's made it to be from the very beginning.

CHAPTER 11 — Sharing Synergies
Shape of a Football

Galatians 6:6 - Those who are taught the word of God should provide for their teachers, sharing all good things with them.

One of the hardest things we struggle with is the constant battle of sin in our lives. The devil is like a mouse squeezing through a tiny hole. Sin is knocking at the door 24/7. How do we keep up with the battles? Sin is like a line of hurdles, we have to leap over it all day. Whenever it is calling your heart, see past it. Look at the crown on the other side. Moses always looked to the end reward, eternal life in the most glorious place. He called it more precious than any treasure ever found. That isn't where our mind turns when we are in the mindst of sinning. I think we need to continually train our minds to be conformed by being in the Spirit. Romans 12:2: *Do not conform to the pattern of this world, but be transformed by the renewing of your mind.*

We need to look at the sin we are facing with a shadow of God behind it. Sin and spiritual warfare will never escape anyone on this planet. It comes on heavy when we are tired and our shield is down. The devil knows that, he is always on the lookout for when we are ready to act. I have a full shield, and am ready for anything at 5:00 in the morning. But, late night after a long day, watch out. I am sure that is what most of us face; we need to be aware of those situations. We always know when they are coming, be proactive. I really struggle when I am alone. The bad thoughts attack my heart and soul. I have always had a bad temper, I know when it may strike. My wife has always seen this part of me. It is the worst part of me.

Someone told me, when you really are at the end of your rope. Just take a deep breath and say Jesus over and over. It always works, if I come full circle back to Him, I settle down and think about who I am hurting. This is our flesh doing this, in this world. No one can escape the flesh, that is where we break down, and the devil knows that. I think that living in the same skin or bucket is the real goal. Don't be someone else in one place and another in a different place. That is my goal in life, to be in the same bucket no matter what the time or place.

I respect people the most who are always the same, they never change no matter where they are in life. I think we need to live intentionally on trying to learn more about God and the word. My biggest battle is being a man, using the computer every day and being tempted by some of the images that kill our brains and our marriages. I know how important it is to avoid sin; one way to avoid sin is by being busy and by being in community. We schedule things on a daily basis to be around other Christians to learn more from each other. Also, just be around good friends it gets our mind off of things that make us wonder. This gets to be a struggle with just about everyone. Part of it is being lazy. A friend of mine said, just the other day have you heard of the seven deadly sins. He read them off to me one after another, lust, anger, gluttony, sloth, envy, pride, and greed. I wrote them down as soon as he finished explaining a few of the ones I didn't understand. I admitted,

I constantly brake those over and over. Being honest is what it says in the Bible if you have one of these thoughts you've committed the sin. That's why I am so thankful for the blood of the covenant in God's promise He forgives our sins.

We would all be in big trouble without that, I do try to not sin every day. But I live in the flesh; in the flesh is what gets us each and every day. We have all fallen short of the Glory of God. I love stories of people who've overcome any type of battle with sin. One of my favorite things at Hosanna, is when they bring somebody forward to tell a story of how they battled something in their life, or how they share a particular story that led to synergies to help them battle their demons. I've also been at fundraisers were people explain their life stories, and explain how they have overcome sin. What I love most is when people explain that they still battle with that each and every day and they turn to God in prayer to battle through it. Those are the ones that I really get the most out of, because people are human and when people admit that they are struggling with something, it makes me understand that we all struggle.

Look at the following illustration:

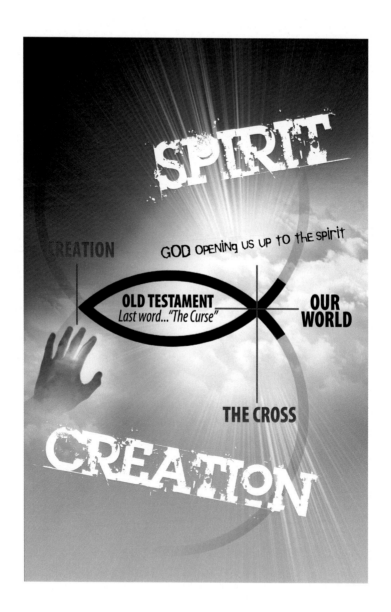

SPIRIT

CREATION

GOD OPENING US UP TO THE SPIRIT

OLD TESTAMENT
Last word..."The Curse"

OUR
WORLD

THE CROSS

CREATION

175

When Rick and I were first discussing how I wanted to show the two circles meeting in the synergies that come in the middle. We ended up also discussing how, we both learned things in the Old Testament, and how there's a lot of stories that don't seem so great. The last word in the Old Testament is "curse." So I really started to look at this and look at these connections and figure out how that works with synergy, and what meaning it might have, of how we live our lives. In part of the synergy that comes out of the circles connecting, is realizing that we are not perfect, and we all have faults. So going back to when I know other struggle, is such an important part of witnessing, we have to paint the picture that we are not perfect. And what you find the more you read about characters in the Bible and especially in the Old Testament, you find that they all struggled.

Look at David and Goliath, it's one of the great stories of the Bible. But once David grew to be king, he was tempted all the time. He committed adultery, he had people killed, and yet he turned to God in the end. Or, when you look at any other character they all struggled, and they all had faults. So when you look at the synergies that come together and meet, I think the most important thing we all have to remember is that we do have faults and we do struggle. Some of the men in the Thursday morning prayer group, joke around about how we are KFCer's. This stands for Knuckleheads For Christ. I know it sounds kind of weird, but to me it opens up that synergy when we all come together, with faults and problems that we've already brought to God. In these faults that we admit to help us break down the barriers that we are all sinners and we all need the community that we share.

I really think that's the most important part of the synergy puzzle, if you don't come to the circle with your guard down, how can you ever expect people to trust you. If you say you're perfect and you don't have problems, how's that possible. Everyone struggles, everyone in the Bible struggled, and everyone forever will struggle. So when you let your guard down, and let people know that you're not perfect I think it opens up that perfect part of your circle that lets others in. One of the coolest things I like to see is when a leader of the church or a mission tells a story of how he or she falls every once in a while. That's when you really get, to that opening that allows the synergy to happen.

When you really start to understand, that it's not about us, it's about others that even opens up the circle more to let others in. I still see people each and every day that don't realize that it's not about them, it's more about helping others and being there for others. I constantly hear people pray for things that they need and things that they want and they forget to ask God to help others. But that's part of the process, I'm not judging them, I just see people at a different point in their relationship with Jesus, and of course that's okay. That is one of my biggest buckets that I need to work on, is not to judge others. If you remember back in chapter 10, he saw the illustration of the buckets, the question mark bucket for me is judging. I constantly judge others, and I'm trying to get better at it, and I pray that God will help me each and every day.

Now you want to open the circle even more, work on trusting one another. The circles that are most open are the ones that you gain trust over time from one another. I think this is the most important part of the circles, for not only improving your relationship with others, but witnessing to others. The trust factor is a number one and part of that is what we talked about earlier being able to let your guard down so others can come in. As you remember back in the earlier chapters when I was talking about being in one of my youth groups. Many of those kids were looking at bad things on the internet when we confessed our sins and admitted our faults. That is what opened up the circle, that is the statement that allowed them to trust me that when I let my guard down they let theirs down to. I was amazed by a few of the kids that just opened up instantaneously at that moment.

That is how we open up the synergy circles, it's not easy. But it is part of the trust factor again how can we trust anyone if we say we are perfect and how do we expect them to trust us. The opening up of the circle, is the only way to allow the synergy to happen. Think of stories you heard, even ones where complete strangers met one another. There is something in there that allows that trust to happen. And once that happens, watch out!

Recently Nicole from our church, was pumping gas at a gas station, and she saw a family ahead of her and the father was in tears standing over the gas pump. Now if you look at the story where does the trust start? Well she asked him if there was anything she could help with? The circle, just barely crept open, and he admitted that he didn't have any money to put gas in their car. She offered to slide her credit card for gas, the man now was in tears of thanks. That circle opened, and his wife stepped out of the car and thanked her also, as the story just gets started.

A few minutes later, she saw two girls sitting in the backseat of the car, and she realized she had clothes from her home that she was dropping off at Goodwill. So she offered the clothes to the two girls. They jumped out of the car and started trying them on right there at the gas station. While this was going on, another man walked up and, observing what was going on. He pulled a gift card from a local supermarket out of his pocket and offered it to the man. Now the circles are expanding within minutes, the trust is there and there is no judging, just love. From that point on, it really started to explode. She got to her office that morning and posted the story on Facebook and hundreds of people "liked" it. That exploded into thousands of people. Fast-forward to that evening there was a man sitting in Ohio contemplating taking his life from some of the problems he had faced in his weakest hour. He read the story, and called Nicole from our church, she answered and the next thing you know he's giving his life to Jesus Christ. PRAISE GOD!

A fast-forward even further, the synergies of circles connected together. Brannon came to Minneapolis, and is going to drug treatment sponsored by some friends at our church. Look at those synergies look at those circles it's incredible what can happen when we just let others into our lives. The circles take off so fast, that sometimes there is not enough time to even look at how they happened. They did, and we know it's through prayer into believing that God is there to help us.

Now once we open the circles for synergy it's amazing what can happen, one of the things Rick and I talk about after this book is published is to create a website where people can drop stories and tell stories about how people do good things for others. There are thousands of stories like this, and I can't wait to hear them all. There are stories like this happening all over the world, and all we ever hear are the bad stories, and how this world is just going downhill. I think we can all change that by listening to the Holy Spirit and using these connections to change it all!

I talked about the Career Connections group that started at our church, and what has sprung from this at Hosanna.

When I look back, that we started the group and we each listened to the Holy Spirit, in each of our different ways to put this group together. It has been unbelievable how many people have found jobs, or just been inspired to try to keep looking. One particular person Audrey was one of the first people to ever come to our group. She was sitting at the same table as me, and was telling a story with tears in her eyes. I felt terrible hearing what she had been through, but she also had hope knowing that God would take care of her and her family.

She continued to tell her story, I was being inspired by how much she trusted God who would take care of her. Once she was finished, she talked about how her chipped tooth destroys her confidence every time she goes in for an interview. That afternoon I called my friend John, who is a dentist, and asked him if he would be willing to help her with her tooth. John did, and fixed the tooth. She was so happy to have that tooth fixed, and she had confidence beaming from her the next time I saw her. About two weeks later she got a job with a big corporate Bank in town. It was a part-time position but she was willing to do it. Since then she's been promoted, and she's doing great.

Just this last weekend we had a speaker at our church on leadership, Joel Canby, the author of "Love Works." So here's Audrey at a leadership conference trying to better herself. I was so excited to see her. I asked her how her family was doing, because I remembered from the first time she came to the group that her daughter had been really struggling. Her face lit up, and she told me that since her jobs, she was able to afford the surgery that her daughter needed, and her daughter had lost 180 pounds. Okay, stop there for a minute. If the only reason we started career connections, was to save Audrey, and to save her daughter through the Holy Spirit then that would've been enough. But you know it doesn't stop there, her daughter is now coming to church, and now getting more and more involved with the church.

So now think of the ripples that, are being sent out from just her daughter having more energy in being more involved at Hosanna. There are dozens of people that are affected by her attitude, and her smile in and around the church. That is where this gets really really cool. That is when you start to realize that God and the Holy Spirit send these ripples out in all different directions. It gets so fun, just to see these individuals grow, and see what they can do for others. Just think, if 1000 churches had one Audrey, and she touched 10 to 15 people, that's 15,000 people that would be touched. That's how these ripples work, now imagine each one of those 15,000 people touching 15,000 people with the Holy Spirit. That's 225,000 people, that's a large city of people being touched, and working with the Holy Spirit. That's what our goal should each be as Christians, just be in the Spirit and figure out how we can help others, just like Jesus did when He was on earth.

It's so amazing when Jesus says in the Bible that you will do more in the Holy Spirit than I did. That's when it sounds like crazy talk, I think, but when you start multiplying these good deeds and gestures like Nicole and Audrey, anything is possible.

CHAPTER 12

Belief in the Mission
Hogan's Heros

John 19:28 - Jesus knew that His mission was now finished, and to fulfill Scripture he said, "I am thirsty."

Sometimes when I think of this #1 knucklehead (me) writing a book, and how much time it takes to write a book, it is just crazy. Did you ever watch the show Hogan's Heros? The show constantly talked about the mission they where on, the mission was their course. We are all missionaries in our own way. We have to be constantly looking at life that way. The mission is our existence each and every day. John 15:8 says, "This is to my Father's glory, that you bear much fruit, showing yourselves to be my disciples." That is our main goal on this earth, is to live each day showing others what a joy it is to be alive in the Spirit. That is living out a life of joy, on the good days and on the bad days. That is one of the most difficult things to do, being alive on the bad days. That is a enormous struggle for me and my fleshly life.

What is the mission, what is your daily mission? The mission is just being better people at loving one another. In Hogan's Heros each of the prisoners had a skill they used in trying to escape from the soldiers. Just like each one of us has a gift in the body of the church. In chapter 15 I talk about Groundhog Day and how some people feel they just keep doing the same thing over and over each and every day. And unless some tragedy or crazy thing happens, we are just going on and on without really any purpose or mission. I think that's part of the growth that we feel each and every day, is knowing we do have a mission on earth and that is to tell people that there is a better way to live our lives. What I'm saying is a better way to live, not telling people how to live their life. I am just showing them the way of Truth. We have to realize God has a purpose for us that He knew before we were born.

One of the things that I really started to notice on the road is how impatient people are when they're driving. Everyone in such a hurry to get places, they're just flying down the road frustrated with life. And believe me I'm not judging these people, I'm just looking at their lives and wondering if it's really worth the stress they go through each and every day. And I'm not saying I don't go through stress, I stress every day of my life. It's just that, when you live under the Holy Spirit and know that God is watching over you, you start to realize how wonderful life can be. I really think it's that Heaven on earth feeling you get knowing that God is taking care of you.

And again I'm not sorry to say that bad things don't happen, they do every day to all kinds of people and not one of us is immune to it. But I am saying that people each and every day to live a better life would just knowing that God loves them. One of the things I'm really starting to understand, is all the characters in the Bible. I'm not even close to knowing each one of them, or knowing their stories. But I am starting to realize that people make mistakes and people had hard days all throughout the Bible. Think of Noah spending 120 years building an ark in the middle of nowhere, he had a mission to build an ark to save the inhabitants of the earth. Can you even imagine the first day when Noah started building it? This ark was bigger than a football field, taller than a 10 story building. If you've ever stood next to a cruise ship, you realize how mammoth they are, and how much skill and labor went into building one. And then to have it float, are you kidding me. And when Noah did this, it was back when there was no electricity, no bolts, no rivets, and no modern-day glue.

He literally put one piece of wood down, and God said it was the exact time to go and gather the wood and build a ship the size of a modern day stadium in the middle of nowhere. Think of how long one year is, then think back 10 years, and now 25 years. Look at that times five, and that is how long it took Noah to build the ark. Can you imagine his frustration and all the problems he ran into each and every day? It must have been frustrated, just thinking about how he was even going to get the wood and supplies for the ark. But to take 120 years, he had to have many ups and downs, thousands of frustrations. Just think when he started building the Ark his kids were babies, and his kids helped him build quite a bit of the ark.

Or think of Abraham, when he waited forever to have a son. Finally in his old age he did have a son, and then God commanded him to sacrifice his son's life. Once again Abraham was going to obey, he followed what God commanded right up to the last second. Then God provided a sacrifice so Abraham could spare his son. All of the stories in the Old Testament are about being on a mission. Following what God commanded and following through for His plan. That is just as much of a plan as the plan He has for your life. Every detail has to happen in order for the ultimate plan to play out, which is the new Heaven on this Earth. Just do what God is asking in your heart, find out how to use your gifts to help others.

I also truly believe there are guardian angels watching over each of us, to protect us and allow us to fill out the plan God has in our lives. I have so many times had things happen to me where I know someone is watching over me. Being part of the mission is for all of us, we all have a special gift to share. *1 Peter 4:10, "God has given each of you a gift from His great variety of spiritual gifts. Use them well to serve one another."* I think finding your gift and using it to help others is the grand slam of all grand slams. If we have a gift and we don't use it to help others, then we are really missing the boat. Don't think your gift has to be huge, it doesn't. Just helping one person with your gift is enough. God will show you how to use it, and how it should be used. We are all part of the body, for His plan.

My son recently hurt his pinky finger on his right hand. He is a good athlete and very gifted at sports with hand-eye coordination. So put your hand out, look at your right pinky finger. Now look at the last two joints of your finger. That area probably weighs .0001% of your entire mass of body. Now that is the part of my sons body that kept him on the bench. To me that is crazy. This boy with strong legs and arms, but yet he couldn't play because of half of a pinky finger. Now think of you and the body of Christ. What if you are the reason the body can't play. Maybe it's the nudge you ignored to help your daughters Powerlife Group as a sub, or maybe you like to mow and the church grounds needs mowing. Maybe it is just being a friend to someone.

I love watching this woman at our church that oversees our ushers and runs communion distribution on the first weekend of every month. I love watching her greet people, seat people, and I especially love it when she runs communion. She is on fire for God and it shows. One day I was walking into Lifetime Fitness, and she was right in front of me. I said "Hey, communion lady?" She turned around with a little puzzled look. I told her how awesome the job she did at our church and how cool it was to watch her enthusiasm for her gift. She said thank you with a huge smile. Then I told her to have a awesome workout and gave her a high five. She gets it, she isn't up there giving inspirational sermons or trying to be something she is not. She is just being faithful to her gift of smiling and making all feel welcome. I guarantee there are several people that have stepped into that church and stayed because of her welcome. This is where you see the full body of the church. It can't run at full capacity without her, and it might even be on the bench without her smiling face.

Now lets say she greets one person that stays at Hosanna because of that greeting they received, and that person joins our church. 5 years later that person is at work and invites a person from their work. That person joins and they hear a sermon 2 years into going, they are inspired by a message to go over seas and help others. Get the picture of how these ripples work and how the body of Christ works. It's really that simple, it's just us figuring out our spiritual gifts and taking one step. I wouldn't be writing this book if a guy named Chris Murray didn't introduce me to a Bible study 16 years a go. That was the beginning of the chain reaction that lead me to the intercession on February 12, 2011. That is what I am talking about, and Chris has a gift of connecting people together. He is really really good at it, and continues to bring people together.

So let your pinky be the part of the body that completes the church. Go sub in a Sunday school class, go usher, or go mow the church lawn. The way I figure my spiritual gift is to think of it in these terms. We will be spending eternity in Heaven, and it clearly dates in the Bible that we will be doing stuff in Heaven. What could you do 24/7 for eternity. I know mine, sharing stories of Gods plan. I also wouldn't mind mowing, I love to mow. What do you just love to do, when you do it time stands still, you could do it forever. Search your heart and get back to me.

That is the plan, God has a plan for you that isn't what you maybe thought it was, but he will find it for you, just watch out for some if these ripples, they turn into title waves. Seriously I have hated reading my entire life, but I do enjoy books on tape. I tell my publisher all the time that I can't even read my own chapters. But I am writing a book. CRAZY Stuff!

I realized why I am writing this book. A guy visited our Thursday prayer group at Hosanna recently. His name was Bruce Thompson and he wrote, "The Handbook of Love." He said something that really made this entire book calling stick. He said he knew he wrote the book to open doors. Wow, this entire book idea now makes sense. There have been so many days that I wasn't sure if this is what I was called to do, but now I know. It will open many, many opportunities.

If a day equals 1000 years, how much time is 1 hour?

1000/24h = 41.66666666666666667
1 hour = 41.66 years
41.66 years = 41 years 7 months 28 days 1 hour 26min 24 seconds

One half of a Vikings game is my 52 years

1 second = 0.01157 years OR 4 days 5 hours 25 mins 26
seconds

1 minute = .694 years OR 8 months 9 days 20 hours 9
mins

2 minutes = 1.388 years OR 1 year 4 months 19 days 16
hours 18 mins

3 minutes = 2.0826 years OR 2 years 29 days 12 hours 28
mins 48 seconds

When I look at these times it is really a conversion table
of how Heavens time vs. our earths time. Think of something
that happened years a go. It can be 5 years or 30 years. Things
that feel like they happened a minute a go. I have a few, both
celebrations and tragedy.

In 1987 the Minnesota Twins won the World Series, I
can still remember that moment like it happened yesterday.
We had just moved into a new house and we had some
neighbors stop over with their excitement. It was really cool
for me because I was a huge fan. I had worked at the old Met
Stadium for 9 years and Kent Hrbek from my high school was
on that 1987 team.

If we look back, that was over 25 years ago now. The
memory of some of those moments is like it happened last
night. 25 X .694 = 17 minutes. That is how long it has passed
in Heaven's time. I have seen two kids go from birth to one
in college and one in high school. But that is my point, it all
travels so fast. There is no way I can remember all the things

that happened each and everyday of those 25 years, it feels like it all just flew by.

In Heaven's time it did, all 17 minutes worth. That is one if the cool things about writing this book, I am realizing Heaven is right here, and revival will come to this place if we all get on the same page. Going outside the gate and helping others, and doing it with compassion and love. When I came up with the title, "There's No Time Like Heaven" I started to realize we are in Heaven if we want to be in our hearts.

Now look at another event only a sad one. Sept. 11, 2001. I remember exactly that day and all the events up to it and after. That was 12 years a go or 12 x .694 = 8.3 minutes in Gods time. So in that time on earth they have built an entire sky scraper on that site. 12 times we have mourned the death of over 3,000 Americans losing their lives at that tragic happening. Millions of people suffering over the loss of family, friends , and part of our freedom and billions of prayers listened to and answered by God. All in 9 minutes to Him.

I just know that in Heaven there won't be pain and suffering. It will be a honor to salute the people of this earth that died protecting and serving. When you stop and think of the time at which God sees things it should make us more patient and spend more time waiting on God and studying Him even more.

It's seems like forever when my friend Jeff passed away. In Heavens time about 3 minutes have passed. He's still walking through the gates and in utter awe of the beauty of Heaven. I know I will be there right behind Him, in a matter of minutes. When you are talking eternity you see the bigger picture. You really start to see the enormity of it all, the universe is expanding and so are we.

Louie Giglio does an awesome job explaining this in one of his talks he gives. Look it up on YouTube it will blow your mind. It's called "How Great is Our God." It really puts in perspective how much time and space we are talking about in Heaven. Heaven is so huge we will never be able to put our minds around it, that's what this video will make you realize.

One area of my walk that gets me 100% covered in joy is when people tell their stories of how they have been changed by Trusting God. In our Agua Viva meetings we call them life stories. I attend these meetings even though I haven't gone on one of these trips. All the people that ate going on the team have to tell their life story.

I am an absolute junkie for these stories. I can't get enough of them, I could sit in a room for 10 hours and listen. The stories are like snow flakes, not one is the same. They are all unique and different. All include at some point reaching for the rope and almost every time there is one person that helps them with that rope. Most if them it is a stranger or even the most unlikely person they can think of in their lives. In another chapter I talk about finding the 5 that got you to the cross. Find them and thank them.

In the life stories people have never seen this person again. Rick who helped me and did all the illustrations for this book is just that person. He was working pumping gas in high school. The old fashion way, where you pump it for the customer. It was just a normal day, when suddenly a girl hangs her head out the window and says "Jesus loves you, have you been saved?" That's it, that is a big part of his life story. Are you kidding me, that's the kind of stuff that makes me explode inside!

Another life story, Chris who went to Honduras last year said he was in the hospital and had zero hope. A woman walked by his bed, a complete stranger and said, "Can I pray for you?" He said that was the moment his ship started to turn around. From hopeless to giving hope back to the people of Honduras. You can't make this stuff up if you tried.

I have always tried to figure out what this book is for, and will one person read it? The other day after 2 1/2 years of fog. Or about half an hour in God's time in Heaven. It all came together, and I called Rick right away. My favorite verse in the bible by far, my life's purpose. Romans 10:9. It is my witness test, five questions that couldn't offend a fly.

1. Do you believe in God?

2. Do you believe He had a son?

3. Do you believe His son Jesus lived on earth and taught us and performed miracles?

4. Do you believe Jesus was beaten, and nailed to the cross and died?

5. Do you believe He came alive and is now back living with His father in Heaven?

That's it. Answer those 5 questions and let God be your judge. Now you be your judge and watch what happens. So out of that Rick and I developed a website called www.10-9stories.org. It is a web site that you can watch 10 minute and 9 second stories of people from all over the world.

It is crazy the visions I have for this site and how it can help others. One of the missions of the site is to teach people with these stories. People are created for a purpose on this earth. That is the mission.

CHAPTER 13 Clarity
Field of Dreams

1 Corinthians 13:12 - *Now we see things imperfectly as in a cloudy mirror, but then we will see everything with perfect* **clarity**. *All that I know now is partial and incomplete, but then I will know everything completely, just as God now knows me completely.*

I love comparing life to movies. I really believe the Holy Spirit can show up anywhere, in a song or in a movie. The Holy Spirit teaches us in everything, good or bad. Same with movies, here are just a few of the messages I have seen. When I went through the experience on Feb. 12th, I started seeing things different. I really started to see how I would see myself in a "Build it, They Will Come," attitude. That is the quote from the movie Field of Dreams. Field of Dreams is one of my favorite movies ever. When I came home from my intercession and knew I needed to get a hold of Jay from Agua Viva. It was like a build it and they will come scenarios, there was work to be done before the mission could happen. At the end of the movie when Kevin Costner says, to his father, "maybe this is Heaven." I think a lot of times that is exactly what it is. It started out in the beginning as earth as in Heaven, and we brought sin into this world and someday you revert back to

Heaven on earth. I really think there are times when Heaven is on earth. Think of those moments, when you're with your family or in a quiet place and you really wonder if this is what Heaven is like, just a sliver of it.

This is what I think we should be striving for, living lives according to God's will helping one another, and being in community and building a real, "is this Heaven?" Just like in the movie, when he asked his dad "Is there a Heaven?" His dad says "yes, it's where dreams come true." Then Kevin Costner's character, spins all the way around looking at his surroundings, and sees how blessed he really is, and what God has given him. He sees a beautiful sunset, he sees beautiful land, and then he spins around and sees his farmhouse with his wife and daughter swinging on the porch. And that's when he realizes, and says, "maybe, this is Heaven." Then as his dad is walking back to the cornfield, he says those famous lines. "Dad, want to have a catch?" which really wraps everything back together that he is with his entire family right then and there.

I think this happens with other movies to, I think there's all kinds of scenes in movies were God puts something in there for us to compare to our own lives. You know I don't think He does, I know He does! Sometimes it's for us just to search out the message. He's trying to get to us. It doesn't have to be in movies He can be in real life, or to meet something that we read, or experience. Or can be a particular story that just trickles out in all different directions. I really think it is when we start seeing things through God's eyes, we put ourselves in those situations. Just like the way we should read the Bible, we put ourselves in their shoes and feel what each one of them were feeling at the time of the story.

About six months after the intercession, I was attending a high school football game, it was a Friday night and I was sitting there watching the game with my wife and friends. Right at the beginning of the game I had a nice conversation with my friend John who did some dental work on one of the people from our career connections group at Hosanna. Her name is Audrey, and he fixed one of her teeth so she could be interviewed for a job. It turned out great, and she ended up getting the job. So there's a real good feeling in the air, a spiritual feeling, and the ripples from just that story go out to a whole bunch of people. As I sat there on this beautiful fall evening, I could just feel how the Holy Spirit was working through the connections in my life.

At half time, I was off to get a hot chocolate and popcorn. Just before I got up, and saw two friends of mine Scott and Merlyn were sitting a few rows back. I had not seen either one of them for months. I been talking to them earlier in the year about possibly going to Honduras, they always asked me when the next trip was, and I was excited to tell them I was leaving in November. So we chatted about it for a few minutes, and then they asked me to come to a seminar at Prince of Peace church in Burnsville, Minnesota the next morning. They said this man Tony Campolo was good to be speaking there, I've never heard of this man but they said he was a really dynamic speaker. I tried to come up with excuses of why I couldn't go, and then I said "well maybe, I will see in the morning if I end up coming."

Now back up to a few weeks before that, or maybe a week before that conversation I had that night. Rick who's doing illustrations for this book, he and I would get together occasionally and talk about the illustrations. Well that week I was thinking about how the circles connect and how were all connected and I was also thinking about in the Bible where it says to one day is to 1000 years. 2 Peter 3:8 "but do not forget this one thing, dear friends: with the Lord a day is like 1000 years, and 1000 years are like a day." So one hour, to God is 41.6 years. So I really thought about this quite a bit, I got so far is to tell Rick how I think there's no time in Heaven. That is how I came up with the title this book, is through that thought. Every time I explain this to somebody, it's hard for them to comprehend what I mean. What I mean is, that there truly is no time in Heaven. Have you ever had the experience of just spending time with people and it's extremely happy or a situation when you know that there's something else going on? Time just flies, I mean four hours can be gone in the snap of the fingers, that is how God sees our time, there is no time in Heaven, that's what I explained to Rick that day.

Now fast-forward to the next morning after the football game. I was driving to see Tony Campolo at Prince of Peace Church in Burnsville, Minnesota. I got there and really surprised Merlyn and Scott by showing up that morning. I researched Tony Campolo, and watched a few of his videos. I thought it was interesting, and I was looking forward to seeing him. Now there's been at least 10 to 15 times, in my life I have been in a situation where somebody is upfront speaking and I literally knew they were speaking right at me. Tony was about halfway through his message, and he started talking about traveling through space. It was so funny, because right when he started talking about this I could feel he was talking to me. Then he started talking about traveling at the speed of light in time does not change when you're traveling at the speed of light. Then he started talking about, that there is no time in Heaven and God's time is right now. He even went so far to say when he gets up in the morning he sits at the of the bed and because there's no time in Heaven. Jesus dies on the cross for his sins each and every day. And he talked about how he lived his life knowing Jesus was dying for his daily sins.

When Tony finished, I was walking to the back of the room with Merlyn and I told him I had this thought in this vision about no time in Heaven earlier in the week and I couldn't wait to write about it in my book. That was the first time I told Merlyn that I was writing a book. He was extremely excited for me, and I told him I have no reason why I'm writing this book. I went through a little bit of my story about the fact that I don't read and that it is just crazy that I was writing this book. But I did really start to think again about this no time in Heaven concept, and I knew with the story with Tony Campolo that God was confirming this in my heart. He wanted me to share it with others. I know I can never go into that place where people have lost really close loved ones, but I have had thoughts lots of thoughts that we enter the Kingdom of Heaven where we are all entering at the exact same time because there is no time in Heaven. Again this is my opinion, but I was truthfully shown this from God and the Holy Spirit and I was confirmed of it a few days later. Literally I was never even going to go sec Tony Campolo, I had never heard of the man. No one was asking me and out of the blue just like that you go to see a public speaker, and in that room I was hearing this message. I know I was being affirmed that there is no time in Heaven. He answered a lot of questions and the more I think about it the deeper it gets. Just like when I listen to an audiobook just recently called proof of Heaven, he talks how time stands still throughout the time he was traveling to Heaven. I know this is a message I'm supposed to bring to this book, I know it with all my heart.

I've even gone so far to having thoughts that when I enter Heaven I will be entering at almost the same moment as my friend, Jeff Barber. I will walk through the gate simultaneously through it with him. And I'm still trying to understand parts and Scripture that will make this come alive. The more I think about this, and the more I see how much people suffer after losing a loved one, I realized that we are the ones that suffer. We are the ones staying back with the sins of the world. The ones that cross through the gates of Heaven, are maybe waiting seconds for us to arrive so they're not suffering at all there. They are just waiting for that split second for us to get there. Again this was just shown to me, but it was so confirmed that Saturday morning. But I'm a true believer in this, but there is one part in the book, "Proof of Heaven" that makes me even think this is more alive, is that when he visited Heaven he flew over earth as it was in Heaven. He never got to go down and see the people on the earth, When I ever do talk to that author, I would love to tell him that I think he was in that "earth as it is in Heaven," and he was on that earth but that's the new earth, the wait will be once Jesus returns again. But it's such a cool thought, to even let your mind go there for a second, that eternity is no time it'll just go on forever and ever and ever and ever and ever. Just like those vacations when you spend time with your family, and you just wish it would last forever. But the coolest thing of all is that in Heaven they will last forever.

That's why it's been more important than ever to ask people to just follow, because that's what you have to do. Share with them what's in your heart and what you believe. I really think the best part, and the only part of sharing the gospel in today's society, is to build up that trust first. People are so wary of false prophets and false teaching, and ways they think there to be taken. I really think that trust is the key factor. I love what Gabe Lyons says, "I been witnessing to my neighbor for years and he doesn't even know it."

We are talking to others dealing with their frustrations of the everyday world. Sometimes we stop and witness to people we love. I think we have to make it as simple as possible. We don't need to make it complicated.

Sometimes it's simple to show people how God loves this world and its people. John 3:16 – "For God so loved the world that He gave His one and only son, that whoever believes in Him shall not perish but have eternal life." In Romans 10:9 – "if you declare with your mouth that "Jesus is Lord" and believe in your heart that God raised Him from the dead you well be saved. These are the beginning baby steps to coming in contact with the Holy Spirit, and bringing your heart and God into alignment. This is where I see a person stepping over that small thin line of understanding that they do love God and they do want Jesus to be part of their life.

I can't tell you how many times I've heard people say, they were witnessing to somebody and they didn't think they were ready. Again that's not up to us to decide, it's for the Lord to decide. When you really look at simply just talking to others, just like when Matthew put down what he was doing and followed Jesus there's a beginning point. Matthew 9:9 - So Jesus went from there He saw a man named Matthew sitting at the tax collector's booth and told him to follow Me and Matthew got up and followed Him. It really is that simple, when you answer these four questions you are on the starting point of following Jesus. When Matthew got up he didn't know anything about what he was getting into but he took that first baby step to follow Jesus.

That is the way I look at witnessing and explaining to others what Jesus is all about, it's just a baby step. When people make the commitment, some are changed instantaneously, and for others it is a lifelong process. I look at this like a scale, from 0 to 100%. When you look at a scale like this, try to imagine where you are, and where your walk is, and remember no one, I mean no one is 100%. We all fall short. In Romans 3:23 - for all have sinned and fall short of the glory of God. So this is what I usually do at this point, is to explain to the person I'm talking to that no one's perfect, but if you truly believe that Jesus died for our sins, He looks at you as a perfect person. And I also tell them, that He can't love you anymore than He does, no matter what you do on this earth, He can't love you anymore.

But it is up to us to pursue Him, we will learn more about Him but He knows everything about us. If you are in Christ Jesus you are not walking after the flesh anymore. That's the bottom line and that is what we need to explain to people. It's a beautiful situation, when we look at life this way, and the way life can be if we quit thinking about the past and start thinking how we can help in the future. I really truly believe this is what God wants us to think, and how we can make this Heaven on earth. The reward is Heaven once we leave this earth, but I know He teaches us if we live the life were supposed to within the boundaries and striving to be more like Jesus, then He rewards us with a life on earth as it is in Heaven.

That is where the real journey begins, that is where we protect ourselves from evil. That is where we finally figure out that there is spiritual warfare and there is a battle between good and evil. And we do pray for protection and wear the armor of God, we too can be provoked and live life on earth as in Heaven.

CHAPTER 14   **Ground Game**
Running the Pass Play

Job 38:6 - What supports its foundations, and who laid its cornerstone

Where do you start with this entire introduction to all the learning in the Bible? I find the more I learn about the stories in the Bible the more I learn about the fleshly temptations all of them went through. I call myself a KFC'er many times in this book, and we have a group of guys at our church that claim that prize too. Knuckle Heads for Christ, which I think is a great name for us. We don't claim to be Holy or anything like that, we just love living our lives learning more about God and His teachings. Just like all the people in the Old Testament, just constantly doing knucklehead things, even though they had seen the miracles of God. I wish more people would just let their guard down and claim the way they are knuckleheads. That is why I am so attracted to Francis Chan's teachings, he is constantly calling out himself as a huge knucklehead.

All of these stories teach about the boundaries that God has laid out for us. But yet it makes us understand how we are so fleshly and we will never be perfect, no matter how hard we try at reaching that goal. I approach it like my sales training. The best quote I have ever heard is, "Information is not a revelation." It great to know all the things about the Bible, but you have to let it work through you.

I saw Tom Hopkins a national sales trainer early in my days of selling. He says become your own sales rep, just take a little from each person and then decide your own style. Don't try to be like anyone else, I think the same holds true in learning how we should be when becoming a disciple for Christ. Just be ourselves, admit our faults and be true to one another. I look at learning the same way, no matter what you hear and stories you hear just learn a little. If it is Tony Compolo, Gabe Lyons, or Jim Cymbala you just hear the stories and learn. Your circle gets bigger, and you expand the kingdom. Let's say I introduced you to a friend of mine from high school. A good friend I trusted, say my friend Todd. I invited the two of you to meet and have coffee without me there. Let's say you met for 30 minutes. Each of you talked about for 15 minutes about your lives. Then after you left I would ask you what you thought of my friend Todd. You would say what a great guy, but I need to learn more and spend more time with him., and I would then ask you. Tell me about Todd's entire life. Tell me everything about him, family and friends and all his stories. Silly question, right? It would take you several meetings and you would have to spend tons of time to find out about his entire life.

That is how I look at our introduction to teachings and the journey of the Bible and the stories. It is an introduction. When we say "YES" is when the journey starts. When Jesus first walked up to Matthew He just approached him and said follow me. Yes that is it, follow me, that is what the introduction to others should be, that invitation to follow Jesus and learn His teachings. It doesn't mean we are going to be living in the

Spirit 24/7. It only means we say yes to the Journey. In some people the journey explodes from there, and they are instantly on fire for Christ, it is a radical transformation that just takes off inside, and quickly fills their hearts in a short time. For others it may be a slow and gradual transformation, and that is OK. We never need to get ahead of God and what He has for our lives. We have to learn and take the first step. Like I said the first step is the biggest, but it might take you a lifetime to get to know what God has for you and His stories that will be played out each and every day in our lives. I am constantly trying to figure out the journey. It is a 3 Part journey:

Salvation - Accepting that Jesus existed and God sent Him to this earth to die for our sins. Asking Jesus into our hearts and allowing Him to start the journey right in your heart. This is a journey that won't be easy and there will be several bumps along the road.

Sanctification – The journey, the road we take to bring us closer to knowing who Jesus is and how He lived His life on earth. The knowing of how the journey of this world began and learning about the many people who gave their lives for a walk with Jesus. Learning to grow with Him, and consistently lining up the buckets of our lives.

Service – Not just service to Jesus and the Kingdom. But service to others and doing it for nothing more than Glorifying God through service with expecting NOTHING in return.

These 3 steps can be an entire lifetime. Some people get through sanctification in a short time. Others are still on the journey in their 50's, 60's, and 70's and beyond. I look at each day learning more about the stories of the Bible and how they apply to my life. The journey to the Heaven on earth moments that is what I have learned the most from my journey. "As Earth as it is in Heaven," having those moments you want to last forever and ever. The moments when you are in completeness that nothing on this earth will fullfill. These are all tied into the buckets from chapter 2. Most people get ahead of the buckets they try to force the service, I see time after time when people don't go through the entire process of sanctification and they jump right into service. Their buckets are inconsistent, and they are headed for a train wreck. One pastor in our community opened his brand new mega church and 3 weeks later announced he was having an affair and stepped down from the pulpit. That is why you have to look at each area of your life before you serve. You need to be ready, well-rounded, full of the Holy Spirit and the Word of God.

I am still struggling with my home bucket; it has been extremely difficult to share some of the stories with my family from this book. We are going non-stop, all the time. I don't mind that, but I am making us slow down and spend quality time together. My home bucket is probably a 3 or 4 right now; I am starting from the core of myself and cleaning out from there. I started with spending less and less time on the internet and computer. Along with that, staying away from the temptations of the things that make our eyes and heart wonder on the web, there are the everyday struggles of keeping our heart focused. Then I am trying super hard with being a better listener with my wife, then following through to be a better husband and father. It hasn't been easy; there is a lot of flesh floating around our home. But it is gradually getting better.

Look at the illustration of the 3 steps. The salvation part is a moment in time, a moment where you speak to God directly. No one can do this for you, it is when you ask Jesus to come into your heart and believe that He will dwell in your heart forever.

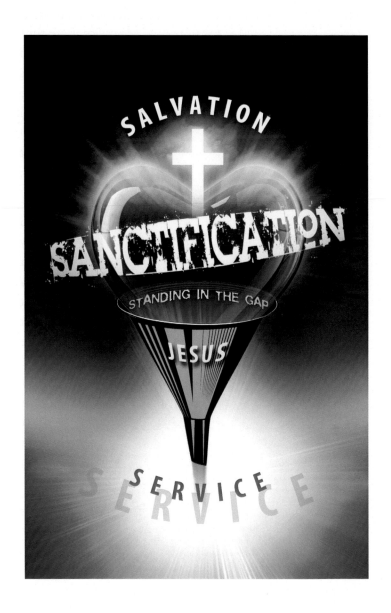

The first step salvation, happens when we turn our eyes to Jesus. When I am witnessing to someone I ask them four questions, but not questions about religion, their past or anything else. Question One is "Do you believe in God?" Question Two is "Do you believe that Jesus lived on earth?" Question Three is "Do you believe that Jesus died on the cross?" And the last question is "Do you believe that He rose again and is living again in Heaven?" It's really that simple, if you believe in those four things as John 3:16 says, "for God so loved the world that He gave His one and only Son, that whoever believes in Him shall not perish but have eternal life." Or Romans 10:9, If you declare with your mouth, "Jesus is Lord," and believe in your heart that God raised Him from the dead, you will be saved. When someone believes in these four things, they have turned their eyes to Jesus. The salvation step is complete. Now it's what they do with it, and how they live their lives. Does it change them to look to Jesus as Charles Spurgeon once said, "turn your eyes to Jesus".

That is the first step to salvation, and I think it's when we really learn to live the Heaven on earth concept. Now it's time to learn the boundaries, to learn from God and His word on what we can do different in our lives. This process is the next step to sanctification. This is where we learn and this is where we both turn our lives inside and out. This is when we will be tempted; this is where you'll find out what we are all about, and how we need to turn to Jesus each and every day. When I first accepted Christ in college, I learned different ways to live my life. I would go months being in the Word and learning new things but then I'd go months completely fallen away. But during the fall away times is when I always learn to turn back toward Jesus, this is where I really think I learned more than ever on how to trust Him.

The sanctification step can take a lifetime. And in that time things can change by the minute. It is all different in our walks, no one is the same. We are all different. We all witness different. Being on the team is the most important part of being a believer. For almost 27 years I mostly hung around on the sidelines. I would get in once in a while. I was OK with that. One of the hardest things to do is to find hope. Hope is one of those things we need to look for; back when my friend Jeff passed away last year it was a very trying time in my life. And then we add Sheila's death and a young death-like Carter's you see the people that lost loved ones. Or my friend Mike and his separation, you just wonder where the hope is?

Then you realize that when you are in these tough times yesterday searching for hope. Hope is always available in the Holy Spirit. That is when we have to dig down and trust. He will carry us through those times. That is the way we must be searching for hope when we go through trying times. We have to constantly trust Jesus and searching for hope in everything we do I know when you're reading this you probably are saying to yourself yeah, yeah find hope in this situation. We have to want it. Christ has it for us is constantly giving it to us with open arms. Hope opens the door of faith and strengthens our love for Jesus Christ.

I really think that hope is one of those things that we need to look at through Christ eyes. He always thought His time here on earth gave us reason for hope. That was most of everything He talked about hope, grace, and love. I look back at some of the tough times I've had in my life and we were always looking for hope. That is part of the whole restoration message; the world looks half-full right now. The world has unemployment, falling home prices, and in a constant battling government. People are getting farther and farther apart in trying to make decisions. As I'm writing this my state, Minnesota is two days away from shutting down. Thousands of jobs will be affected, and the Fourth of July holiday will definitely change for many people.

There are many athletes who want the ball in the final minutes of the game. The ones that always want to take the last shot. We all know these friends are athletes that constantly want to be the one with the ball in their hands. That is how we all have to think, we have to want the ball in our hands at times like this. Find your passion/gift from God and use it to make this world a better place. For some it might just be organizing a food drive or running a food self.

When we traveled to Florida to visit my parents a few years back, my daughter needed to do a service project. So my mom found us a food shelf that some retired people from their community ran. When we were there dozens of people stopped in that morning to pick up a bag of food. Many where at the end of their rope, had lost a job or single parent that couldn't feed their children. Every one of these retired woman just loved on them and handed them the food. The woman could have just been in their retired homes, living a good life. But they chose to set up this food self and help in the community, and like anyone who finds their sweet spot for helping others, the retired ladies said they got more out of it than anyone.

That's where restoration prayer and hope comes in, praying for a resolution is what we have to be doing as Christians. It could be a resolution in a marriage, a resolution to find a job, or resolution to help a child that's not listening and turning away. That is where we have to be seeking hope. This is also where your circles of influence come into play. There is hope in your circles, your church friends, your family friends, or your trusting friends. The circles will give you hope, and their prayers will help to get to them. Just doing things in community and serving others is how we will find it, not at having more stuff, but helping others.

God wants you to have hope in every part of your life. Let your friend's help you find hope, and let your heart consume it. This is the reason for restoration; hope is the reason for restoration. I also watched the video lately by Louie Giglio, if you haven't seen him speak or if you haven't seen his YouTube videos look them up he is awesome. He refers to Ezekiel chapter 47 and how we need to be transformed for the different rivers and going deeper in the Holy Spirit and in God's Word. He has one video called the kiddie pool, we are asked to take a plunge. He looks at the salvation, sanctification, and service in a much different way. He brings the kiddie pool up on stage, and he stands in the kiddie pool and he talks about how most Christians are stuck in the kiddie pool and are too scared to move closer to God.

It's almost the perfect example of how God wants us to grow, that is the sanctification process. I know we can be stuck many many many times in our lives. We can be stuck easily in a rut and don't find the time to learn. But I really think it all comes down to, making the time to step out in God's kingdom. It will be done on earth as in Heaven, I don't think we can reach this without going through the sanctification process. It's a lifelong journey of learning and growing in community and our spiritual lives. I get up every day, hoping I will learn something new, and hoping I will have the guts to step out in faith. As Louie says it's not easy, it never will be easy, but then what is. It takes hard work and persistence. Louie quotes Thomas Edison in this video. "Opportunity is missed by most people because it is dressed in overalls and looks like work." I love that quote, it really makes you think about how hard it is to get things done. God wants us to use our hands and feet, He's the mighty one that put all this together, He can build a star in the snap of a finger, He can perform miracles in the blink of an eye. But He wants us to use our hands and feet, He wants us to do the work so we can learn from the trial and tribulation of doing it.

So many people are looking for this to be handed to them, but that's not how God wants us to do it, He talks about hard work and dedication many many times in the Bible. One of the best lessons I learned when I was in Honduras was how hard we had to work. Every day we woke up, no shower little food using a pick axe and a shovel. That was it, no Internet, no cars, no heavy machinery, just our hands and feet and a jug of water. That is how we got it done, building these trenches to bury pipe to bring bottled water to the community in Honduras. It was a real lesson nothing gets done without our hands and feet, we get so lazy in the United States with all the equipment we have, and all the conveniences that help us get through the day. We forget how hard work really is, but it's a God who wants us to do it. I live in Minnesota, where we can get upwards of 15 to 20 inches of snow one or two times a year. I use my snowblower, to get the snow off the driveway, it's fun and it's easy. But just imagine if I had to do that, with a shovel and no power equipment. A couple years ago we had a heavy snow/rainstorm and my wife and I had to clear the driveway with shovels. It was hard, it took time, but it had to be done, and it's very rewarding when you do it to completion. That is how it is when we struggle when stepping out and being obedient to God. It's not easy, it is a struggle, but it's extremely rewarding.

When I think back on that trip, not one second do I think about the hard work I did each and every day. I think most about how cool it was to not have the chaos of everyday life back in Minnesota. To just be working hard, and helping these people fulfill their dream of having water in their community. Think how silly that sounds to us in the US, we take for granted every day we turn that spicket to get a glass of water or to take a shower. Think how rewarding that would be if every day we did that, we knew that we dug miles and miles of trenches by hand to bring that water to us each and every day. That's the reward, the reward of working hard learning more and more about Christ, yes making mistakes along the way. But learning each and every day.

I look back at some of the times on that trip, I specifically remember the first day I was up on a hill digging a trench with my Honduras work partners. Sweating away in 95° heat, and wondering what was I doing there. Stopping every few minutes to take a break and get a drink of water, while both of my Honduran work partners, one older than me were kicking my behind in the work they were creating. But I know that they were motivated by the reward they were getting and at the end of the day, the completion of the project. That's how we should see things each and every day we are learning stepping out to help God's ultimate plan. None of us know what it is, but we know from learning and teaching that can be wonderful. I look at the same thing, living water is what we should be striving for, learning praying and loving one another.

That's what it's all about, being in the sanctification process, and growing each and every day. And we are to make mistakes, hundreds and hundreds of mistakes, and we all will fall short. We have to realize that is part of the learning process. Falling short and learning from our mistakes is what

God wants us to do. Like I said in one swoop He can go down and perform a miracle and people would be bowing to Him. He wants us to have faith and grow through the use of our hands and feet. That's too easy, and that's not the way He wants us to grow His kingdom. He wants us to live and grow each day, learn from one another and love one another. It's the last thing He said to the disciples, before He left this earth was love one another with all your heart and with all your soul. That's it, that was His main goal of being with us on earth. So we want to be more like Jesus, we have to learn to love one another. And I know it's hard, to do that with everyone. Each and every day I try to strive for this but I fall short. But I do feel the sanctification I'm going through I am learning to do this, and to be the best person I can each and every day. I think the support of friends and other believers is extremely important. We need to connect those circles constantly to re-charge our engines. I have felt some of the enemy attacking at certain times, and the prayer groups, Bible study groups, and honest friends can make all the difference.

I look at it like a NASCAR race when a yellow (caution) flag. Once in a while you need to get new tires and gas up. We all need our down time and we need to keep our engines running smooth and clean. The other pit stop should be a daily devotion; I listen to that internal clock that says I need rest. Then I meditate on what the meaning of what God is trying to teach. Our just reading a few Bible verses a few times a day, really diving in and finding the deep meaning of the Word. Sometimes it comes from other places, sometimes it comes on talking to somebody on the phone or listening to a radio station. You read a few chapters, I talk about how God created everything on this earth, we can find good things in everything we see. I take a few movies that I've seen over the years and really see how different scenes and different things can touch us. That is what's neat about this creation we live on, we can be surprised hundreds of times a day at work, He could show us, we just have to be looking on a daily basis.

The final step, service, is when you've been through the sanctification process of learning from Jesus and from the Word and the ups and downs of everyday fleshly lives. And this is the calling you get to serve Him, I see many times when people get ahead of the time you serve Him when you are not ready. I seen it over and over, and I can almost sense when I know it's not going to work out. But other times people are fooled by the service. There are many stories, pastors, and other leaders who think they're called in service, but yet they're not ready. They get on the service and things break down from something that they just haven't brought to Christ. In these fallen times He will teach us that we need to be 100% ready for the service that God calls us to. That is the affirmation process. I believe that there are things that we want to do, but we have to pray for it to be affirmed by God. It is a Scripture, or through friends, or other means when you know it's completely from Christ. There are many times and I wasn't sure if I was supposed to write this book, then at different prayer times I talk about some of the things that I was writing then. Every time it was affirmed, by the story I would tell, or what I think was possible.

That is what's so neat about living in the sanctification process. I'm not ready for service, but am ready to write this book. When I still look back at the very beginning of sitting in that room and not knowing what was going on, but also realizing that Jesus was calling me to help my friend when he was in need. Yet coming out of that moment, and realizing that there was a purpose for that morning. Only God knows what the ultimate purpose was, but I do know one thing. I wasn't looking for what happened, but as my friend Michael says, deep down I probably was. The ground game, the sanctification process, is the most important process after salvation. Sometimes, I struggle with the warm and lukewarm Christian analogy. It says in the Bible that if I live a lukewarm life Jesus will spit me out. I think that's telling us, is that He wants us to live a life that is in pursuit of pleasing Him. It is not a double life full of sin, and full of being someone we are not. It's the buckets that I talk about in the book, it's about being consistent throughout our lives.

When I look at a scale from 0% to 100% I asked myself what will I need, to not be lukewarm. No one can answer this question because once they answer those four questions: Do they believe in God? Do they believe Jesus walked on this earth? Do they believe that Jesus died on the cross? Do they believe that He rose from the dead? They might be at .01%, someone else might be at 85%, and isn't that okay everybody grows at a different rate. The key is like Spurgeon said as long as they have their eyes on Jesus, and their eyes are not fixed on this world. Which can happen all the time, this world is a nasty place full of distractions. So it's not for us to judge but only for the ultimate judge to be the judge. I once heard someone say they were witnessing to a person telling him the gospel, and the man wasn't ready to give his life 100% to God. He stops short there and didn't explain the rest of the gospel to him, none of us can give our lives 100% to God. All we can do is completely be looking at Jesus all the time, and that is all He asks. Just focus on Him and the teachings and all the rest will eventually fall into place.

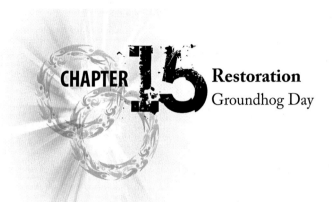

CHAPTER 15

Restoration
Groundhog Day

Isaiah 44:26 - But I carry out the predictions of my prophets! By them I say to Jerusalem, People will live here again, and to the towns of Judah, You will be rebuilt; I will restore all your ruins!

Restoration, what does it mean. The dictionary defines it as an act of restoring, in instance of restoring or being restored, or estate of being restored

Have you seen the movie Groundhog Day with Bill Murray? The movie is about this guy who wakes up in the same day over and over. Daily when his alarm clock goes off Sonny and Cher are singing the same song. No matter what Murray does, he is stuck in the small Pennsylvania town reporting on the groundhog on Groundhog Day. The day just keeps repeating itself and finally he realizes why not make the most of it. Still there are days he's frustrated and he goes crazy. Finally when he finds true love, he begets them out of the grind of the daily life. It's a little like our world. Have you woke up and feel that you're totally caught in Groundhog Day? Like each day is the same thing, and just piles on top of one another.

The world just flies by and we are constantly seeing the weeks just fly by. My parents always said, "Wait until you get older, time really fly's by then." They were 100% right. The weeks just fly by, so why not just adjust your life by 2% to add something for restoration. As our youth leader Luke says, why not try to do something for eternity today. I stated this earlier in the book. Are you going to do something for yourself today or even to do something for eternity today. That is exactly what restoration is, to making a difference in this world so you can really feel good about it. Back in the first couple of chapters, in chapter 6, I talked about being provoked. When we are provoked, it is usually into something that we can handle. Something that we are familiar with? NOT! I look at writing this book, I don't read, and I sure don't write. But, I do have a passion to spread the gospel in a very simple manner. A way that some people won't agree with, but that is ok.

I know I am not a writer, but I know I need to put my story down on paper. I know that God wants me to share it, and witness to others what it is like to get on the field when we are asked. I know that others will help me write this story once it is started. Once you are provoked to do something in the Kingdom, try to figure out what gifts you have that will make you passionate. Really, it doesn't take a lot of effort to figure out how you can help. The first part of help is to figure out three things you are really good at. I call it the "What are you God (good) at?" Name 3 things that are your passion.

Finding your gifts is how we will restore this earth each and everyday. *Ephisians 4: 8 – When He ascended on high, He took many captives and gave gifts to His people."* Now, think about it. These are things if you spent extra time doing them, you would love the excitement and results it would bring. Lets take for example a woman in Nisswa, MN that owns a yarn shop in this tiny community in northern Minnesota. This is what she did for restoration. She loves her little place where she sells supplies to make quilts. She has hundreds of connections through the shop. She teaches others to learn how to make quilts and helps them to know Jesus as Lord.

We must have faith that Jesus paid the penalty for your sins by His death. When you admit you are a sinner and place your faith in Him alone for forgiveness, you will be reconciled to God.

There's a number of ways that people spread the goodness of God's heart. When they do spread these things out I see them as ripples, similar to the circles connecting to one another but ripples that extend out in all different directions. When you look at these ripples they intersect one another and they continually go out. Look at the diagram below and get a sense of what I'm trying to explain:

Think of a time when you did something or touch somebody's heart of the ripples just spread out in all different directions. I can see this over and over in stories of the Holy Spirit. If I look at the day I got out of the whirlpool and went to the intercession, let's just take one arm of one of these ripples. When I ended up meeting with Jay and going over ways to help Agua Viva I started to get involved with Agua Viva and ended up going to Honduras. Since then three teams have been to Honduras and back. With every one of these teams I have learned things and told stories from some of their testimonies. Take for example on last year's trip a gentleman named Chris went on the trip, and I probably told parts of his testimony 50 to 60 times the following week. I know some of those stories from his testimony touched other people and motivated other people. I don't know where those ripples went but I assure you that people understood the power of the story.

The same thing happens when I hear other peoples testimonies or when I'm at PTM or at Prayer Force. One of the things I have realized to, is that when people really release and let their lives be controlled by faith in God they realize good things can happen. This recently happened with a few friends of mine that went out and got jobs that was the job they really wanted, but they were doing it for God's glory. Like a friend of mine Dave, who struggles with trying to find a job for over a year. He finally took a job that wasn't perfect but he knew he had room for advancement. He prayed about the new job every day and trusted God would take care of him. With this company, he ended up moving up to a marketing position almost twice the pay where he originally started. Where he was blessed by some really interesting people along the way.

I know a lot of people that are building tents. "Building Tents" is what we saw generations back, just doing something to make ends meet. They are just doing jobs that aren't their perfect choice, but are perfect for this economy. My dad worked 3 jobs when I was a kid, and I just recently took a minute to thank him for providing for our family when I was younger. But during these jobs they are learning to listen and learn more about God. When I have taken the stories and brought them into career connections at Hosanna and shared with people there how friends of mine are building tents. Let's say one of those people decided to take a job, and they are rewarded with the promotion like Dave's. Then they end up telling some friends about the story, and they to go out and find a job making tents.

Several times at Career Connections at Hosanna people tell stories of how they are listening to the Holy Spirit and being faithful to seeing what God has for them. They stop worrying and start using their hands and feet to make their lives better. They do this process without complaining or telling others how bad they have it. They are continually thanking God for what they have and praising Him for all the blessings in their lives. This is when the flood gates really start to open, when the Holy Spirit comes alive and starts working in them, I have seen these stories over and over.

It is so fun to just sit back and watch. They happen when people just release the worry to the Holy Spirit and just put complete trust in God protecting and watching over their lives. Seeing is believing, the real stories happen when people are honest and they trust. I have seen people become the person they want to be, they still have everyday issues. We do live in a broken world, but their gifts start to come to the surface and shine. This is the beginning of restoration in the lives of believers. When each live is restored than the entire world can be restored one person at a time, in God's time not ours. That's what restoration is, lives being set free through truth and complete trust in the one God of the universe.

These are like ripples that are just sent out through the Holy Spirit. But then I like to really look at a deeper picture, as I go back in the diagram what would've happened if I didn't get out of the whirlpool. It is the same effect that God is putting on these people I know they are "making tents" right now. When I went to Career Connections, where I met Sharon and the other staff. They help others in our church to find jobs. I wonder if I would have met some of these people through other connections? It is cool to look back and see the connections of the ripples that go out in all different directions. I believe these connections are eternal, and we will be discussing these connections for ever and ever in Heaven. My opinion is, when the Bible talks about singing in Heaven; that is when we will be sitting under the mango tree telling each other the stories that helped God's ultimate plan. Also I think of, what about if no one would ever touch my heart. Would some of these connections be made today? I look back from chapter six about planting seeds. I think if I didn't listen to the witness of those people that planted seeds in my heart, when I've been in the Bible study with Mike, which put me in the prayer intercession that day on February 12th. No one knows but God, He has the ultimate plan and He knows our past, present, and our future.

I know that God has a plan for me, and I am just living my life day by day. He will use my gifts where they are needed. I love to listen to different speakers and teachers. Some of the stories they tell are so similar to the walk I have been experiencing. When I listen to Francis Chan I can really relate to some of the things that have happened in his life. I know the things that happen are not coincidence; they are really things that God is directing. Like a movie director He is running the show, and there will be an awesome ending. An ending that brings restoration closer to this place we live, or maybe it will just be the beginning. I know it will happen, if we just keep living the way we should, and helping and praying for one another.

That is were this really gets fun, when you start to look at these ripples in all different directions. I know right now there are 200+ people that have an effect on me every day and how I live my life. And without the support of those people I don't think I can live the spirit filled life that I do today. As I talked about this in Chapter 9 on planting seeds, it really makes us understand how others have influenced us. That's what makes it so crazy, to think about those five people that planted seeds in my life, now think about the five people that planted seeds in each of their lives. I wish I could sit down with those 25 people, that's five each from each individual. Some of those 25 would probably be back from the turn of the century. I wish you asked them who influenced them, and brought them to Christ. That is how the Holy Spirit works in their lives. That's what's so neat about these ripples, these ripples cut through space and time. Let's take for example one of the five people that were part of my life. One of the five seeds that got me to the cross was my friend, Bob, who I went to High School with, at the time I didn't see it. But, I now realized that our friendship was based on God's principles. Sure we made stupid mistakes, but who's counting.

We sat down to have coffee and find out my other seeds. I know as a pastor's kid his parents were very influential on the spiritual life he has today. Let's just take his father, for example, where did he grow up and who influenced him? Was there one person that really really brought the attention of Christ into his life, or was it his parents, or even better was that one moment in time?

Now of his five people it would probably bring you back to the mid-to late 1800s. Maybe that person saw Spurgeon give one of his many thousands of sermons during that time. Maybe that was the person that brought him to the Holy Spirit. And then brought Bob's dad to Christ, which then brought up Bob in a wonderful Christian home. And now Bob is leading a congregation, and having an influence on hundreds of lives. That is where it really gets crazy, when you really stop and think about these ripples. How many people has Bob touched in his life of ministry, how many people are going to hear a story on any given Sunday that might bring them to the altar. That is what really blows your mind, these ripples just carry out and carry out which I believe are the main thing that are carrying out God's plan.

We talk about pastor, Pastor Bill, who was called to start our church Hosanna in Lakeville, Minnesota. He talks many times on how he went out knocking on doors. I started my business, from scratch many years ago and I did knock on so many doors in order to get my business started. So that's what I can really relate to, is the loneliness of making those door knocks, it is one of the most lonely places you'll ever be. And while you're doing that temptation and avoidance hits you every minute. So in Pastor Bill's talks about when he used to knock on doors it really hits home with me. Now fast-forward to 2012 we are expanding our church right now and added on a retirement home and we are also building a new prayer chapel. On Wednesday nights I am involved with some of the team coaching for the leaders. And there are Wednesday nights we have between 1500 and 2000 kids in the building. And I think back to those days when Pastor Bill would be knocking on one or two doors, and the ripples of the stories that have built up to this point. This didn't happen overnight it didn't happen in a split second, it was tons of patience to get at this point. That's the main thing, is realizing that these repercussions these ripples might go unnoticed, it might take years for the ripples to take root and reveal fruit.

Think of the labor that went into building the Hoover dam, the people who put up concrete day after day hour after hour. Football field size blocks of concrete that took not days but weeks to drive. The water was still flowing around the dam and not being stopped when it was being built. But gradually the wall was built, the wall to hold trillions of gallons of water. You couldn't see this being done on a daily basis, but you knew after hours and days and weeks and years of hard work it would be completed to stop the water. Then one day they plug up the holes and formed Lake Mead. This took years of planning, labor, and tons of sacrifice to complete the project. But now look how it supplies electricity to the turbines for generations and generations. It's just like restoration, you don't know what you're doing when you help out at that home, help out with the groups of children, or maybe just go collect cans at a local food shelf. The ripples, can go out in all different directions, and sometimes you don't even know what you're doing, or if you're helping anyone.

That is where the trust comes in, the trust that God is watching over us in helping us in taking those ripples out in every direction. My daughter and I wanted to help at a food shelf down in Florida near my parents retirement home. There are several families that came in tears and thanked us for what we are doing. We were only there for one day, many of these women have been there for years. The satisfaction of helping it seems that people make you feel very good about the place in the world we live. But we'll never know if one of those families have a child that didn't starve that day, or maybe the mom told a story about a young girl that was helping her out at the food shelf. And that child, heard that story and wanted to give back. Once a family is back on their feet, maybe she decided to work in a food shelf, maybe she started a food shelf. We will never know, but let's say if she did and that food shelf helped another family that had a child that survived another week. That child was touched by the story and the ripples went on and on from there.

We've all heard the stories over and over about the ripples that just go out when we help one another; this is restoration at its finest. Stories of helping one another and being in community that is what gets me more excited than anything on this journey we are all on. I think that is one of the many blessings, that really change this from a Groundhogs Day, to a day on earth as it is in Heaven. And then the stories that you hear, they come out are incredible. I think social media, can be a great way to share the stories and help restore this place that we call earth. As earth as it is in Heaven is something I will live by each and every day. It's bringing Heaven to earth through the stories in the ripples of restoration. I pray each day that the stories will continue to touch people; we plan on starting a book connected to a web site that just has these type stories in them, to help people fight through their own Groundhog Day.

This has an effect on everyone, if they are following God or not. The world needs to hear more stories about how we are connecting with each other to make the world a better place. This is where the rubber hits the road, where people start to get contagious to helping others. A feel good story of helping one another is what motivates people to search for more, and to believe there is more to life. I love to see the restoration, and connect with others to build circles that just feed on one another. People have so many opinions and so many ways they look at the world. A ton of people right now think the world is spiraling out of control. You can look at it however you want, that is your right as a person. When you look at the stories that connect us together and the hope for one another, that is when all that stuff goes away.

Restoration is that place where you forget about all that stuff, and you just focus on what this world could be, living in that place called, "Heaven as it is on Earth." I am striving to get there, though improving my buckets and looking for the good in everyone. It's really, really hard sometimes to make this work, but there are days it just falls into place. Sometimes when I least expect it, but mostly when I look for Gods work in everything in every day. That is what gets me so excited about this life and the hope for restoration.

CHAPTER 16

In Heaven
As it is on Earth

Proverbs 16:9 - A man's heart plans his way, But the LORD directs his steps.

Matthew 6:10 - Your kingdom come, your will be done, on earth as it is in Heaven.

One of the coolest things about this book, is the name came to me "there is no time like Heaven" way before I ever knew the meaning of the book. I really didn't understand what it was all to be about, but now that I've written this book it's kind of a twofold answer. On one account it's about restoring earth to Heaven like a place and in the other it's knowing that the Kingdom of Heaven has no time and when we get there we will realize it's all about eternity. It is happening in just one person and one day at a time. It's trying to be patient and alive. A life that shows and teaches us how to live, to NOT JUDGE but just love one another. Now as you see how the circles big or small are going to help restore God's Kingdom, can you imagine if every Christian lived their lives to make God's Kingdom showing what it was meant to be. The thought of the linear line of creation – Ever falling life

– fall – resurrection – restoration is the main way we live our lives. Not just worrying about yesterday, today, and tomorrow. Matthew 6 talks about just getting through today and stop dwelling on the past and never worry about tomorrow. We need to start thinking in circles, about helping others and being there for others.. That is how our Kingdom in Heaven works. It is a circle, not a line. Heaven never ends; it keeps going in a never ending circle. Now imagine your circles with one big circle around it that is your connection to the eternal Kingdom.

It says that, where 2 or more are gathered, He is with us. If that is true, then when He is with us, He brings Heaven to earth. Have you ever been in one of those moments, where you feel like the word of God is directed right at you? Or when someone is speaking, you feel that you are the only one in the room?

When I first thought of bringing Heaven to earth. There is no time like Heaven, because there is no time in Heaven. There are no clocks; everything is a second, a minute, an hour, a day, a week, a month, a year and so on. They all are the same. Time does not move in Heaven. Therefore, Jesus died on the cross over 2000 years ago. And we all see that as a long time ago, but in Heaven there is no time so that happened in the present. In the moment. If you look at time in Heaven like that, then we are all pulled into His Graces at the same moment. Moments in Heaven are not measured in time; it is just one big circle of non-stop time.

This is hard to grasp at first, especially if you have lost a loved one. But we all enter Heaven at the same time, we don't worry about the past in Heaven and we don't look into the future. We just praise God continually and sing His name. My opinion is that we see our circles in Heaven; we are surrounded by the ones who we loved and interacted in Heaven. This is some really forward and radical thinking, but it answers a ton of questions. Why people die when they do, it has a purpose or a story on earth. In Heaven it all happens at once, we are in a no time continuum, that lasts forever. That is why when you look at people that died; we question why they died a certain age.

Time confines us; we never have enough of it. Have you ever been on vacation and said, "I wish this would last forever." That is what Heaven will be, except the vacation will never ever end. Our earthly bodies are always obsessed with time, we never get enough. It Heaven we won't be in that time bubble. No time hence, we all enter at the same time. I believe the circles we have created for God's glory will be there for us to feel and live. The relationships we created will be expanded in Heaven.

I had this thought one day and explained it to Rick who did the illustrations in this book. He agreed with what I was saying, but it really makes you think in a deep state. I was trying to wonder if these where thoughts from the Spirit or just me thinking out loud. Then a few days later I was at a high school football game. I said hi to a couple of friends, Merlyn and Scott. They invited me to a speaking engagement at their church their next morning. I tried to come up with several excuses not to go, I tried about 5 or 6. Finally I felt compelled to go. When I arrived I was taken aback by the location, it was the same church where my friend Jeff was laid to rest a year earlier. When I walked in I was greeted by my friends. The speaker that morning was a man I had never heard of Tony Campolo.

When I sat down, I sat next to my friend. I enjoyed the stories and the way he presented the gospel. Then it happened, he talked about the time factor in Heaven. He explained it exactly the way I did. That there is no time in Heaven, it is eternal. Never ending, and that there truly is no time in Heaven. Tony took a short break and I turned to my friend Merlyn and explained to him my thoughts. I also told him that I had just explained this exact explanation to my friend Rick the week before. God wanted me there, in that place to hear this to confirm my beliefs. He also confirmed the title of the book.

This concept of Heaven solves so many questions that people have of dying and grief. If there is no time in Heaven, the cross, our deaths, family's deaths all happen the exact same time in Heaven. I know this is so hard to grasp, because we live on earth where everything is measured in time. I think the moment we pass over the threshold to Heaven we all go in at the exact same time. That means when we do pass over into the afterlife Heaven is complete to were Jesus is returned back to the earth in earth as it is in Heaven. So at that time we will be living in a place called Heaven on earth the new Kingdom.

In Revelation Chapter 21 it says, "then I saw a new Heaven and a new earth; for the first Heaven and the first earth passed away in there is no longer any sea." I think this is where we pass into, the new earth as it is on Heaven. When I listen to the book "Proof of Heaven" by Eben Alexander I figured that when he was flying over what he thought was Heaven on a butterfly he saw the future of how the Earth will look in the new Heaven. And I really think that's why the butterfly didn't land he didn't get a chance to see up close who was on earth/Heaven. And I really think that is why we're the ones that suffer when friends or family and loved ones die, because we are left on this earth full of sin.

And when you look what Heaven can be like, the perfect place, in the perfect time in reuniting with love ones it will be awesome. Like the movie "Ground Hogs Day" explains, it shows us how much we could accomplish if we could stop time compared to earth's time. Can you imagine if time had stopped, and each and every day we had full sunlight and never had to sleep, how much we can get accomplished. That's what I believe Heaven will be like, living in community with no tears, no sorrow, no fighting, and just love for one another.

Just let your mind wander once in a while, and realize that we are just seconds away from being there, and living in eternal life. I can't wait till I get there, I still love each and every day on earth and experiencing the things God has for me, but it is cool to think about a place like that, a perfect place that is 10,000 times better than we can even imagine. And I think we will also be living in space that is chosen for us, a place that is nicer than any house we could ever imagine.

One of the things I really look forward to is the community of Heaven. Also, being with my family. My wife has been the best part of my life, and I get to spend eternity with her and my kids. I also believe, that we're reunited with people we've lost, as soon as we step through the Gates of Heaven. That also includes children we have lost in the womb. Keri and I had a miscarriage in between our two children, and I firmly believe we will be re-United with her in Heaven. I never thank my wife, for the blessings she has poured on me over the years, but I could never thank her enough. Both of my kids have been huge blessings. Each has their own world they live in, but both have blessed me in so many ways. They are both followers of Jesus and that is all we can ask, for them to have Faith. I once told my daughter, that if she was Taylor Swift with all the money and fame I wouldn't be as proud of her as I am for the faithful walk she has taken. I am also grateful for my parents who have raised us with a Christian foundation that has really taken off.

Both of my kids have been a huge blessing in each of their own ways to Keri and I. Can you imagine the feeling we will have when I get to meet another child of ours in Heaven. To me that is such a cool thought, and one I am so looking forward to, especially the blessings and the rewards we receive in Heaven.

I look back now, a year ago. I have taught we all need to have a Saul moment. In Acts 9 we learn of how Saul was a persecuting believers and God came to him and told him "I am Jesus, whom you are persecuting," He replied. Now get up and go into the city, and you will be told what you must do."

I know that is the moment I had, He said for me to get out of that Whirlpool on February 12th and He spoke to me and it has changed my life. I only hope that the fire stays in me for as long as I live. There are times I don't feel like writing or speaking to others of the stories that God has put on my life. Other times Satan just pounds me down and tells me I am not good enough to be out there lifting up God's Kingdom. But that is part of being in the flesh; we will always have those feelings and battles. Also the temptations in this world can be overwhelming. We need to love God and keep asking for His protection.

The great news is that over 2,000 years ago Jesus lived among us, was tempted like us, and died for us. That is what I always go back to, there is not one person that will ever be perfect on this earth, and we have all fallen short of the kingdom. Then one man walked this earth and taught how we can overcome these sins and transgressions with one commitment. That is asking Jesus into our hearts and telling Him we believe He lived and died for our sins.

This is the free gift, we just have to ask. When I look back at the last year, it has been a crazy ride. I still have a ton of work to do in my spiritual walk. My family is the biggest step I need to take. But just like a person who just accepted Christ, it takes time and energy to learn and to walk with Christ in all areas of your life.

The baby steps to be closer to Christ take time, years. I look at my son when he started playing basketball at 3 or 4-years-old. He couldn't dribble between his legs, or take 3-point shots. It took learning and practicing day and night. Just like our faith, it takes time, but once we take that first step, the journey just begins. It is not going to be easy, and we will face many struggles. But walking with Him day and night is how we learn.

Once we learn to walk with Him, we learn that Heaven can be one Earth. "As Earth and it is in Heaven." There really is no time like Heaven.

We can live the daily blessings, by living our lives within the boundaries of God's rules. That is what the 10 commandments are—boundaries.

Now that I have seen the concept of time in Heaven, there isn't any time in Heaven. I have realized when we accept the fact that Jesus came to earth as God's only son, and died for our sins. I realize that this is a journey. The best part of the journey knows we can have "As Earth as It Is in Heaven Moments." That is what this walk is all about. It is realizing that God has given us gifts and we need to use them to build His kingdom and to have those FAITH moments. That is what we get as Christians, we not only get the assurance of being in Heaven for eternity, but we also get the moments here.

There is a seen at the end of the movie "Field of Dreams." Kevin Costner is talking with his dad for the first time. His Dad asks, "Is this Heaven?" and Kevin Costner answers, "No it's Iowa." Then his Dad says I could have sworn this was Heaven? Costner answers, maybe it is as he looks out at the sunset and pans back to seeing his wife and little girl swinging the porch of his farm house. He has a FAITH moment. He realizes that only being in that moment is like being in Heaven.

The other thing he asks his father, Dad is there a Heaven. He answers, oh yeah. "It's where dreams come true." The ending of that movie sums up more than anything, being in God's grace is where Heaven is. I love seeing things through the beauty and perfection of God's eyes and heart. We have to be looking for signs of Jesus everywhere we look. That is what a FAITH moment is, we start to see them more and more when we look for them. I look at my life's journey and the things that happened both before and after my experience on February 12, 2011. I don't know why that happened to me, and why God chose me to write this book. I do know that my circle of life and understanding it is widening.

I look at today and all the blessings we each have in our lives, a week ago a strong storm hit the east coast. It was a few weeks before the 2012 election. The news was explaining how over a million people were going to be without electricity for days. I thought about that, and it was a tough stretch for those people, but it was a bump in the road compared to the third of the world that has never had electricity. Then it made me think of my trip to Honduras over a year a go, and how I realized how good we do have it. But, it can be better with this realization that the Holy Spirit can carry you through the tough and the good times.

I look back at that week I spent in Honduras and the theme of this book, we are all knuckleheads and we all make mistakes. But God takes people from all walks and backgrounds. I think of the group that started Agua Viva, 4 guys chugging along in a small Bible study group. Then a man named Frank started thinking and wanted to do something with water—to give the world living water. For weeks Frank came to the group with this message on his heart.

They thought, how can a small group of 4 guys from a small town in Minnesota make a difference. Well Frank never gave up and Jay, Loren, and Dave listened. And you know me, as stated in chapter 6 about the seeds I want to know who the 20 seeds are in these 4 lives? Because they will be thanked in Heaven. There is another team down there as I write this story. To date 17 communities have been blessed with water to their door, now only water living water. I considered it a privilege, to be involved with Agua Viva and be able to watch individuals grow throughout each one of the trips. That's the funny thing about helping others, you think you're helping them, and don't get me wrong you are, you get way more out of it than they ever well. Every time I talk to people that come back from one of these trips, they are so amazed by the people in the stories that each trip involves.

Mary, one of the people that went on the trip when I went, has an amazing story. She raised two great boys for many years on her own. She struggled and many times she had the look to the Holy Spirit for help. Once her boys were growing and she was very involved in church, and very involved with raising money in garage sales, in dinners for Agua Viva. She decided to go on a trip, and it just so happened to be the same time I went. When Mary showed up for the 12 meetings and introduced herself she was very nervous about going to Honduras. She was also very nervous about being too overbearing for the group. I thought it was funny when I first heard this, and I planned to stay away from Mary on this trip. The Thursday morning before we left, 4 of us from the mission trip came to the Hosanna prayer group to bless us.

It was really cool. They prayed over us, and specifically asked for the Holy Spirit to be with us on the trip. When you ask these type of prayers, be prepared for what's in store ahead. We had a great trip, that involved blessings, healings, and several types of personal answers to prayer. We all got along great. Mary's worries of overpowering and nervousness never happened. One of the most amazing things that happened was that Mary, who thought she was just going on a one-time trip to check where the money she raised was being spent, ended up going the next year. Since then she has sold her house and her car, left her job and now she lives in Honduras. It's just amazing what God will do when you ask for the Holy Spirit to intervene in our lives.

That is what makes living in community, and learning more about our relationship with Christ is all about, we never really know what's down the next turn, but we can trust that will be the right one. I try to live my life loving others, and treating people the way I want to be treated. I definitely fall short of that some of the time, but I am trying to get better each and every day. By trying to be a good husband, a good father, and a good friend to everyone I come in contact with, each and every day. That's what I think is so cool about Jesus and the last thing He did on earth, He could have preached, He could've changed the course of time, but no, He stopped and humbled Himself and washed the disciples feet, each and every one of them.

He wanted to show us how important it is to love one another, and be a servant to one another, in order to make this place called earth a better place. Time has passed, from the minute Jesus left this earth until now. You look at people and you think this place has really become a crazy place to live, and it has but it doesn't always have to be that way before looking to love one another and just trying to live a life of loving one another.

When I look at the purpose of this book, I have no clue. But to sum up my experiences of the walk I have had with the Holy Spirit, it makes me wonder what is it all about, can we each make a difference. The answer is yes, I was in a meeting at church last Saturday for the unemployed. I talked about this in chapter 5 when the Spirit worked through a few of us to bring this group to back to life at Hosanna. We were wrapping up the meeting and we were making some closing comments. Al a guy who attends, he is one of the easiest going guys you will ever meet says, "Go to work with the attitude you are helping the company be a better place. Don't do it for you, do it for the company." Can you imagine the work envoirment in any country if that is the attitude we had, wow it would be on fire for each other.

We need the same attitude towards God, and look to Him each day. If we look at our daily lives, get up every day learning about the life of Jesus and His teachings, and figure out how you can make God's Kingdom a better place for His glory. That is the master plan, figuring out how we can help in that plan that God has for each one of us. Then we join those plans together, to make His giant plan to fulfill His promise of coming back in restoring this world to a perfect place. That is when I look forward to forever and ever. What is ever and ever, it's hard to comprehend. But like my friend Mike once said, if a bird takes a grain of sand from one beach here on earth and flies it to the moon. Drops it on the moon, and flies back to earth to the same beach and picks up one more grain of sand and flies that back to the moon. Imagine if this bird takes this trip over, and over, and over again millions of times. Then wait until every grain of sand on the earth is distributed on the moon. It would take billions and billions and billions of years and everlasting life is longer than that, so that is why I choose to follow Jesus and look forward to Heaven.

When I look through what I've written in this book that there is no way I am at all perfect in any manner. When I look at the buckets back in chapter 2, I need to still work on each one of my buckets. I really want to work on being consistent all the time, home, work, and with my friends and family. Especially my home bucket, that's the one that needs the most concentration, and the most dedication to really making sure I work on filling that one to the brim. I am trying to be the same person all the time: at work, home and church. I know I need to wake up every morning asking the Holy Spirit to show me ways to fill each one of these buckets, hopefully I will be there someday. I strongly suggest to you to find your seeds as I talked about in chapter 9 (planting Seeds). If you can't figure them out, then email a friend like Bob and let them know how important their faith was from the beginning. Then start thanking them for what they did in your lives. It's eternal that is for sure. It's that simple, and ask the Holy Spirit for help and guidance and watch what happens!

Psalm 46:10
He says, "Be still, and know that I am God;
I will be exalted among the nations,
I will be exalted in the earth."

God doesn't need us, but we sure need Him. When we say yes we see that He has a plan to use our hands and feet to help Him fulfill His plan. He has a plan for the world if we are on the bus or not. I choose to be on that bus, hopefully you will too. It is up to each of us to figure out how we can be in that plan. Figure out your gift that you have to offer God. Yes, we all have something to offer, and we have to figure out that gift.

One way to figure out your gift. We all agree we are going to be living life of eternity. The bible states we will actually be working in Heaven. We will all have a part in the community in Heaven. The lord will restore us back to the garden (Heaven) Genesis 2:15, The Lord God took the man and put him in the Garden of Eden to work it and take care of it. I love to mow, I know that is what I love to do.

I will be mowing in Heaven. I also love to tell stories, and I know I will be sharing my stories in Heaven. All of the ones that glorified Him, and others will be the connections of following His ways that connect each one of us. This, to me, is so simple. I'm just glad I realized it so I can be on His team forever.

When I look back on writing this book, I still cannot define exactly its purpose. When I try to come down to the root of it, I think it is just the baby step we need to all take to figure out what we can do to make this a Heaven on earth place. Meaning to love one another just a little more, by being prompted to get out of our chairs.

That prompting can be to start a fundraiser for a non-profit, or to go mow the church lawn. What you will find when you do get prompted and you do follow it up, then to tell that story to others to get them to do the same. I am a true believer that we do get prompted by the Holy Spirit each and everyday.

Like the cover of the book, when we do tell these stories in humility, people get energized to get up. That is the forming of the circles. Those circles collide with other circles and explode into a place we can all love in, I think that is the restoration that is possible.

I love movies, and I can bet you can find good in all kinds of movies. Field Of Dreams is one of my favorites. Throughout the movie Shoeless Joe asks, "is this Heaven?" And Ray always responds, "no it's Iowa." One of the last lines in the movie Rays dad asks "is this Heaven?" Ray says "no," then Ray asks, "is there a Heaven?" and his dad says, "oh yes there's a Heaven. It is where dreams come true."

After all the struggles, and judging Ray had gone through, Ray looks all around him, his wife and daughter, the beauty of the field and farm. He turns back to his dad and says, "maybe this is Heaven." That is the point if this book, if we live our lives doing things that prompt us with love and NO judging we can bring Heaven to us for brief moments.

There are many times I have done a Ray in my life. I look how blessed I am, and thank God everyday. Trying to use my hands and feet to make this earth a better place, one story at a time. Matthew 7:7 says, "Ask, and it shall be given you; seek, and ye shall find; knock, and it shall be opened unto you."

I think this is true restoration, on earth as it is in Heaven....

Go find your gifts.

WEBSITES TO VISIT

www.goodnightshepherd.com

www.aguavivaonline.org

www.faithslodge.org

www.worldservants.org

www.10-9stories.org

www.worldencounter.org

www.rivercitypress.net